The Yes Men

The True Story of the End of the World Trade Organization

To our parents

Copyright © 2004 The Yes Men

Published by The Disinformation Company Ltd.
163 Third Avenue, Suite 108
New York, NY 10003
Tel.: +1.212.691.1605
Fax: +1.212.473.8096
www.disinfo.com

Design & Layout: Matt McElligott & Jean Dahlgren

Library of Congress Control Number: 2004093374

ISBN 0-9729529-9-3

Printed in Mexico

Distributed in the USA and Canada by:
Consortium Book Sales and Distribution
1045 Westgate Drive, Suite 90
St Paul, MN 55114
Toll Free: +1.800.283.3572
Local: +1.651.221.9035
Fax: +1.651.221.0124
www.cbsd.com

Distributed in the United Kingdom and Eire by:
Turnaround Publisher Services Ltd.
Unit 3, Olympia Trading Estate
Coburg Road
London, N22 6TZ
Tel.: +44.(0)20.8829.3000
Fax: +44.(0)20.8881.5088
www.turnaround-uk.com

Attention colleges and universities, corporations and other organizations: Quantity discounts are available on bulk purchases of this book for educational training purposes, fund-raising, or gift giving. Special books, booklets, or book excerpts can also be created to fit your specific needs. For information contact Marketing Department of The Disinformation Company Ltd.

Disinformation is a registered trademark of The Disinformation Company Ltd.

disinformation®

10 9 8 7 6 5 4 3 2 1

Table of Contents

acknowledgments

This book was written by Andy Bichlbaum, Mike Bonanno and Bob Spunkmeyer, and was designed by Matt McElligott, Jean Dahlgren, Sarah Collins, Olya Szyjka and Juliann Van Wormer. The events described in this book were acted out in real life by the first two above. That was the easy part: without our numerous friends and helpers, none of this would have happened.

The most basic and essential support has come from the people of Thing.net (Wolfgang Staehle, Walter Palmetshofer, Darrel O'Pry and Gisela Ehrenfried). Bravely and without the least complaint, Thing.net has housed our server for the last five years, providing us continuous virtual existence in the face of outrageous corporate bullying, including a shutdown of the entire Thing.net network in response to a Yes Men prank against Dow. The Thing.net story merits an entire book in itself.

Along the way we have been lucky to receive useful financial support from entities such as Creative Capital, the Alpert, Guggenheim, and Langlois Foundations, the New York Foundation for the Arts, the Lynn Blumenthal Memorial Fund, and Rensselaer Polytechnic Institute.

A small group of international trade lawyers in Salzburg, Austria were able to learn about the far reaches of WTO policy thanks to the help of Ryan McKinley, Jordi Claramonte Arrufat, James Baumgartner, Hans Bernhard and Lizvlx.

Television viewers of the world were able to watch the WTO express its true feelings thanks to the help of Brian Holmes, Nathalie Magnan, Jean-Marc Manach and John Reed.

We could not have shown Finnish commerce how to control foreign workers without the brilliant visuals of Patrick Lichty, who has always translated our ideas to the visual realm with unerring weirdness and accuracy, nor could we have lived without the brilliant and nightmarish costuming of Sal Salamone, or the intellectual and moral support of Juha Huuskonen, Juha Hytonen, and Fred Royer.

Enabling us to leave a strange taste in the mouths of the hard-working students of Plattsburgh, New York, were Richard Robbins, Marco Deseriis, Caz McIntee, Rich Pell, and Andrew Lynn, not to mention the reliably lunatic visions of Patrick Lichty and Matt McElligott.

For their invaluable help in the sad but necessary work of dismantling the WTO from Down Under, we are forever indebted to Hélène Georgeault, Leah Grycewicz, Deborah Kelly, Zina Kaye, Josephine Starrs, Leon Cmielewski, Ian Walker, Dave Gravina, Enda Murray, Mr. Snow, Sumugan Sivanesan, Katie Hepworth, Ali Benton, Jean-Michel de Alberti, and especially to Barry Coates and the World Development Movement.

```
tml><head><meta
TP-
UIV="content-
pe"
NTENT="text/
ml; charset=UTF-
><title>Google
arch: pie </tit
><style><!body,
,div,.p,a{font-
mily:arial,sans-
rif }
v,td{color:#000}
,.fl:link{color:
f6f6f}
link,.w,a.w:
nk,.w a:
nk{color:#00c}
visited,.fl:
sited{color:
51a8b}
active,.fl:
tive{color:#f00}
 a:link,.t a:
tive,.t a:
sited,.t{color:
00}
{background-
lor:#bbcced}
{background-
lor:#249}
{width:33em}
{color:#249}
.i:link{color:
00a08}
.a:link{color:
08000}
{display:none}
```


Neither Andy nor Mike studied economics in school. We know very little about the subject, and we won't attempt to convince you otherwise; if you are of sound mind, you would see through us immediately. Yet to our surprise, at every meeting we addressed, we found we had absolutely no trouble fooling the experts—those same experts who are ramming the panaceas of "free trade" and "globalization" down the throats of the world's population.

Worse: we couldn't get them to *dis*believe us.

Some of our presentations were based on official theories and policies, but presented with far more candor than usual, making them look like the absurdities that they actually are. At other times we simply ranted nonsensically. Each time, we expected to be jailed, kicked out, silenced, or at the very least interrupted. But no one batted an eye. In fact, they applauded.

How did we do it? It was easy. We have no special talent for this sort of behavior; on the contrary, we may be particularly ill-suited for it. Our middle-class upbringing leaves us feeling awkward in the presence of the captains of finance and industry. Our bohemian inclinations make us look forlorn and out of place in business suits. Also, Mike and Andy both have ancestors who were systematically slaughtered in the last "major" war, making us extra touchy in places like Austria. Finally, neither of us has much acting talent.

One thing we do have going for us is regular internet access and some knowledge of HTML. Another thing we have on our side is a certain amount of leisure; being the underemployed idlers that we are, we had the *time* to do this. Finally, we were somehow

WORSE: WE COULDN'T GET THEM TO DISBELIEVE US.

Identity Correction

As many readers will know, "identity theft" has become a major problem on the internet: scoundrels intercept personal information like your date of birth, residence, and credit card numbers, then have all kinds of fun at your expense.

What we have done is the opposite: we have found people and institutions doing horrible things at everyone else's expense, and have assumed their identities in order to offer correctives. Instead of identity theft, *identity correction*.

Our career in identity correction began in a very roundabout way. (In fact, we didn't even know at first that "identity correction" was what we were doing—Bob had to point it out after the fact.)

In 1993, while still in school, Mike spent a few furtive months performing microsurgery on talking GI Joe and Barbie dolls, switching their voice boxes so that the GI Joes would say things like "Math is too hard," while the Barbies would bark "Dead men tell no lies."

The dolls were returned to toy stores, along with a note providing a number to call "if you experience problems with your doll." The numbers actually belonged to TV news desks, who then received

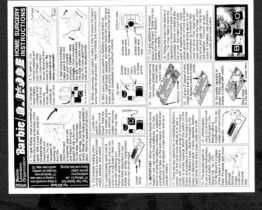

11

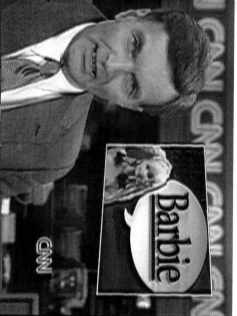

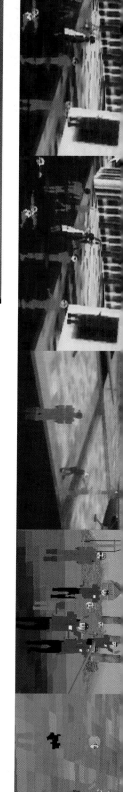

calls from troubled kids. Each reporter also received a mysterious video featuring an inside look at the "gender transformation laboratories" of the Barbie Liberation Organization (BLO). The action provoked a firestorm of media coverage, from *60 Minutes* to *The Simpsons*, and from Seattle to São Paolo.

Three years later, Andy found himself hired to program the little people that ran around on the screen in an action game called SimCopter. Bored with the concept, he secretly created an army of men wearing nothing but swimsuits, who from time to time popped up and showered each other and the player with kisses. Eighty thousand copies of the game were placed on store shelves before the company noticed the "feature," upon which it promptly showed Andy the door. A chance remark to a journalist friend resulted in the kissing boys being featured by media all over the world, from network TV to *The Wall Street Journal* to the *Helsingin Sanomat*.

Andy was amazed to discover just how easy it was to get international press attention for an activist cause. Figuring that far smarter things could be done with a little forethought and planning, he formed ®™ark (RTMark.com), an anonymous website featuring a "sabotage stock market" on which activist pranks were listed, discussed and

Bay Area programm

COMMUNITY NEWS

by Dennis Conkin

A renegade computer programmer at the East Bay software firm Maxis unloaded an unexpected feature on the company's new flight simulator game that got him fired: muscular, bikini-clad men who periodically appear and kiss each other, according to Maxis.

"It's the subversion of a child's play," and said there was no way his software company to

(allegedly) funded. To get the ball rolling, Andy gave himself $5,000 and reported the "anonymous investment" to a few journalists; the Simcopter stunt became ®™ark's first "success."

One success, however, does not make a market. Word reached Andy of Mike's gender-bent dolls, and he sent Mike an e-mail asking if maybe, just maybe, this ®™ark thing had funded the Barbie Liberation Organization as well. Mike searched his memory and recalled that it had, to the tune of $10,000, and a long and fruitful collaboration was born.[1]

[1] Our first "real" action, in mid-1997, was to publicize a compilation of pirated and recombined Beck songs by anti-copyright label Illegal Art, by sending to thousands of journalists a corporate-style press release with the title "®™ark Finds Bucks for Beck Rip-Off." A lawyer at Beck's record company quickly riposted. "Bragging about copyright infringement is incredibly stupid," he said—an admonition reproduced in 30-point type in the *New York Times*.

®™ark also promoted "World Phone In Sick Day," helped coordinate a "Floodnet" attack on the Mexican government's webservers in support of the Zapatistas, and "sponsored" various other actions. At one point, invited to an important Austrian art festival that was awarding a $10,000 prize to the movie *Titanic*, ®™ark used its position to create a consolation prize: $1000 to the fishing village that the *Titanic*'s special-effects filming had wrecked. (See RTMark.com for more on these episodes.)

Project by project, our team grew to include Patrick (animation), Matt (graphics), and Bob (editing, ideas, real-world experience).

Our first venture into identity correction proper came in 1999, as then-Governor Bush was revving up the campaign machine that would eventually propel him, with the Supreme Court's help, into the White House. A fellow named Zack Exley had had the foresight to register the domain name GWBush.com, and he offered the domain to ®™ark as a cultural investment.

Bush's real site, GeorgeWBush.com, claimed that Bush had been the ecology governor, that he would be the education president, and so on and so forth. Bush was clearly in need of some big-time identity correction. Our GWBush.com ended up looking almost exactly like Bush's own site, but featured different highlights from Bush's career: the decline of Texas to the status of most polluted state in the union under his stewardship; his repeated and abject failures at business ventures; his refusal to deny that he had taken cocaine, while thousands of Texans languished in jail for the same crime; and, in the "Genealogy Fun" section, his grandfather's ties to the Nazis.

We were so successful at correcting Bush's identity that the Governor himself took note of our work. His campaign threatened us with legal action for copyright infringement, complained to the Federal Elections Commission that we ought to be required to register as a Political Action Committee, and spent over $4,000 buying up names like GeorgeBushBlows.com, BushSucks.com, and so on. Finally, asked on live

MATT   PATRICK   BOB

14

television what he thought of the site, Bush gave a characteristically articulate reply:

"There ought to be limits—there ought to be limits—there ought to be limits—to, uh, to freedom. But, uh. And we're aware of the site, and this guy's just a garbage man, that's all he is. And of course I don't appreciate it, and you wouldn't either."

Bush's sadly prophetic gaffe generated articles about our site in hundreds of newspapers and magazines, and on TV and radio worldwide. Identity correction was a hit.[2]

Our entrée to the high-flying world of international trade came six months later, and in exactly the same way as GWBush.com: through a stranger's e-mail. This stranger, one Jonathan Prince, had heard of our identity correction work for Bush and thought we could do the same for an equally (if more abstractly) onerous target. Just two weeks before the WTO's "Ministerial"[3] in Seattle, which thousands of demonstrators would disrupt, he offered the use of a domain name he had thought to register two year before: GATT.org.

[2] Another of our attempts at identity correction was YesRudy.com, which made important corrections to the public identity of then-New York mayor Rudy Giuliani. Giuliani, unlike Bush, didn't respond, dooming the site to obscurity after a few articles in publications like the *Village Voice* and the *New York Times*.

[3] The WTO calls these meetings "Ministerials," in part because it is government ministers that attend, and in part because it sounds important.

15

ANDY MIKE

WTO DG Moore deplores fake WTO websites: They "undermine WTO transparency"

WTO Director-General Mike Moore has severely criticized recently-created websites which mimic the WTO's websites and create confusion among the public. He says the WTO welcomes criticism and change, but is concerned that the confusion created by the fake sites with their misleading Internet links is a disservice to the public. This could disrupt a much-needed debate by making WTO information more difficult to obtain.

This is the text of his statement:

I am deeply concerned about the recent appearance of anonymous websites which copy important design features of the WTO's official websites. This causes confusion among visitors looking for genuine information from the WTO, disrupting a much-needed democratic dialogue. It's illegal and it's unfair to those who have a genuine case in criticizing the WTO, an organization that only functions with the authority of sovereign governments.

"By creating confusion, the fake websites are interfering with the public's ability to obtain information from the WTO. They have copied the WTO website's design, and they use domain names such as "www.gatt.org" and page titles such as 'World Trade Organization / GATT Home Page' which make it difficult for visitors to realize that these are fake pages. Whereas

To be honest, neither Andy or Mike knew what GATT might refer to. But Bob did, and so did Jonathan.

The General Agreement on Tariffs and Trade was the international free-trade agreement negotiated after World War II which provided the framework for the expansion of corporate power across the "free world." In 1995, the WTO was formed to administer and enforce this agreement, as well as new ones such as the Global Agreement on Trade in Services (GATS) and the Trade-Related Aspects of Intellectual Property Rights agreement (TRIPS).

The WTO and the agreements it administers may sound banal and benign, but they are neither. Just as "freedom of the press" has turned out to be a great deal "for those who own one," "free trade" has been a wonderful thing only for those who own or control a transnational corporation. For "free trade" elevates the freedom of transnationals to do business however they see fit above all other freedoms, including freedoms that are crucial to the vast majority of the world's people: the freedom to organize a trade union; the freedom to grow your own crops; the freedom to maintain social services or protect the environment you live in; the freedom to *eat*, the freedom to *not* eat certain things, the freedom to drink water. In one form or another, all of these rights are under attack by huge corporations working under the veil of "free trade," this mysterious right that we are told must trump all others.

THE WTO SAID IT "DEPLORED" GATT.ORG AND ACCUSED US OF "CREATING CONFUSION."

Despite the fact that the old GATT has been superseded by the much more powerful and wide-ranging *WTO*, people often mistake one for the other—a fact that Jonathan had the foresight to think might be useful to those of us in the business of public-service identity correction.

There were seven days left before Seattle. Andy worked feverishly to create a version of the WTO's website that would more honestly explain what the WTO was about. At T minus 2 days, it was ready.

The WTO was not amused. Although the WTO's website and spokespeople never mentioned the thousands of people filling the streets of Seattle to protest its policies, it chose to devote a complete press release to our website. The WTO said it "deplored" GATT.org and accused us of "creating confusion," "undermining WTO transparency," etc.

The WTO had given our site just the boost that it needed, like Bush had done when he announced his opinions on freedom. Without the WTO's help, GATT.org would surely have remained a simple satirical website, as we had intended. As it was, we were able to send out a perfect David-and-Goliath story to our list of 10,000 journalists, resulting in dozens of newspaper and magazine articles, all of them mentioning the criticisms we heaped on the WTO. GATT.org's search-engine rankings shot through the roof.

Now perhaps GATT.org could be called a fake, but it was a very obvious one. Anyone with half a brain who actually *read* any of the text Andy had written would immediately know it could not possibly have been written by the real WTO. But apparently many people

Will the Real WTO Please Stand Up?

If you saw a World Trade Organization spokesman behaving oddly—saying strange things about trade or wearing an inflatable golden phallus—don't be confused. Its probably just Andy Bichlbaum, the WTO impostor.

An American living in France, Bichlbaum, 35, belongs to the Yes Men, an anti-globalization group devoted to "representing the

Last summer, for instance, he was invited to speak at a textiles conference in Tampere, Finland. Presenting himself as the WTO's Dr. Hank Hardy Unruh, he praised slavery, decried Ghandi, and called the American Civil War "the least profitable war" in U.S. history. Then he stripped down to reveal a skin-tight body suit, pulled a ripcord, and inflated a three-foot-long phallus, the "Employee Visualization Appendage," he explained, a device to allow managers to control workers through electronic impulses.

Bichlbaum has also "represented" the WTO at an international law conference in Salzburg, Austria, and on CNBC Europe last summer, advocating "justice vouchers" for "countries that commit heinous human rights violations, but want to stop." He says he plans to strike again this spring. "Somewhere in Oceania."

Yes Men remove "deceptive" copyrighted materials from its Website. But when the WTO posted a warning about the hoax on its home page, a tweaked version soon appeared on gatt.org. "A fake WTO Website—www.wto.org—has been created to deceive Internet users," it read. "The only official WTO site is www.gatt.org."—Jerry Useem

Bichlbaum isn't an international-trade advocate, but he plays one on TV.

WTO more honestly than they represent themselves." Two years ago the group took control of the Web address gatt.org, where it put up a home page nearly identical to the WTO's. Because it is easily mistaken for the real thing, the Yes Men receive a steady stream of e-mails intended for the WTO—including speaking invitations. Bichlbaum is only too happy to oblige.

Would you be foo

from the world of big business have less than half a brain, don't read, or both, because we were immediately flooded with email from lawyers, ministry officials, academics, and assorted others who—thanks to a quick search on Google or Yahoo—all thought they were corresponding with the big shots in Geneva.

We answered these emails with great care. Many of the messages we received contained difficult questions about obscure but critical WTO rules, yet we were always answered with enthusiasm and the most searching honesty. Others included formulaic well-wishing from august representatives of WTO member countries; these messages too received the most careful handling. (We find these e-mails so instructive that we have included many of them on our website at www.TheYesMen.org.)

Finally came the messages with requests for speakers from the WTO to address important international conferences on global trade. And that is how the Yes Men were born, and how, in appearances before erudite audiences around the world, and even on prime-time television, the WTO came to make a decisive break with its white lies and outright falsehoods of the past. Over the next three years, the WTO was able to publicly show its true face without shame. Eventually, it was even able to recognize its past mistakes, shut down, and reorganize as an entity devoted to making governments and corporations act responsibly, humanely, and in the interest of all people everywhere.

WORLD TRADE ORGANIZATION

● **About the WTO**
● Site Map
● Search

Registration
Français
Español

WTO Director General Mike Moore explains that free markets lead to better pay, and better pay cleans up the environment: "Every WTO member government supports open trade because it leads to higher living standards for working families, which in turn leads to a cleaner environment." (*The Toronto Star*, October 12, 1999)

Brazilian AIDS drugs a sure path to economic sickness

The Bush Administration correctly argued that Brazil must no longer manufacture proprietary AIDS drugs in violation of U.S. drug company patents, even if this will mean removing 100,000 Brazilians from treatment rosters. The U.S., calling patent enforcement a form of "tough love," insisted that the number of lives lost to AIDS in the short term will be dwarfed by the number saved in the long term through a more efficient medical products market. Read the special bulletin.

A new Holocaust

Much has been made lately of IBM's participation in the Holocaust. Indeed, IBM proactively and creatively helped the Nazis identify all of Germany's Jews, which in turn made possible one of the biggest slaughters of all time. Today, however, another Holocaust is taking place: it goes by the name of "distrust of big business," and it is every bit as terrible as the last. Read the report.

The bright side of efficiency

In all the hullabaloo over IBM's wartime behavior, the benefits of industrial automation have been slighted. Indeed, automation has given nutrition corporations the ability to replace outmoded means of food production throughout the Third World with new, massively efficient and profitable methods. And the increased reliance of these developing economies on First World corporations has meant some valuable new lessons for their populations in times of financial lack. Read the report.

Trade Topics:
ods
vices
llectual Property
vironment
logical Property
velopment
gionalism
de Policy Reviews
pute Settlement
ocurement
ctronic Commerce
view Procurement
perty Research
mmerce Reviews
search & Analysis

Resources:
O Ministerials
-line Bookshop
cuments on-line
gal Texts
dia Newsroom

HACKTIVISM

...are acting up online. By David Cass...

WIRED BLUE YONDER

Subversion, Inc.

RICHARD R...

Through anonymous videos, art actions, and anti-corporate mutual funds, ®™ark reaps cultural divide...

gally) available from ®™ark for $29.95 through their website. "$29.95 is a perfect example of what ®™ark was designed for..."

Y2K?

®™ark.
vok.rtmark.com

Inside the Game of E-Mail Hijacking

Look-Alike Web Addresses, Run by Foes or Pranksters, Can ... ...ent Missives

EL PAÍS, jueves 4 de noviembre de 1999

COMUNIDADES

...eotypes,
...oxes of

Busí campaign Net real estate

Bush buying up

...staff...

■ Internet: Strategist fo... GOP front-r...

RUDY
GIULIANI
U.S. SENATE

"Welcome to the Rudy Giuliani for U.S. Senate Web Site"

...

El grupo de a...

A la izquierda la página oficial de Guiliani; a la derecha, la ...

Etoy Batting ...

'SimCopter' becomes 'HimCopter'

Gay programmer fired for

...founded in 1996 and put up its Web ...

...ists were being muzzled ...

when as many as 50,000 copies hit retail stores
Maxis, makers of the popular game SimC
may face even bigger troubles. Servin, whose
was to help create animation for SimCopter, ...

...e to release a
...ecial occasi
...s birthday, ...

May–Jul '94

THE POP LIFE

CREATIVE CAPITAL

1,810 Artists Seek Grants From a New Foundation

By JUDITH H. DOBRZYNSKI

To judge by the exp
new cultural support
many of the nation's
clamoring for financial
these prosperous times.
By last week's dead
Creative Capital Found
round of grants, applic
1,810 visual, performing
artists had flooded into
wich Village office of the
...ation was form...

Creative Capital will disperse ...

Mischief Exec

...corporation pranksters ha
...—and it is them.

...SLOGAN "CORPO-
...E consulting for
...e twenty-first centu-
conjures images of
industrious young
crafting media-
...ding campaigns,
...p ingenious new
...d using the word
...verb. And in-
...ategists behind

RTMark
organizat
motto be
ize in suc
in an inc
fashion.

Most re
ficially sp
pronounce
name is a
trademark

[E-mail]
ELECTRONIC BUSHWHACKING

From an e-mail message sent in April to college
students who inquired about internships after visit-
ing www.gwbush.com, a Web site that appeared to
he maintained by the George W. Bush Presidential
Committee. The site was actually run
...fessionals "dedicated to
...uch re-

Tweaking Beck With Piracy

LOS ANGELES — It's not what
you do, it's who you do it to. That's
what a group of musical mischief-
makers on the Internet are discover-

Toy terrorist gives less
in hijacking headline

DEREK MCNAUGHTON

RUDY
GIULIANI
U.S. SENATE

A Special Message
from the Rudy Giul
Web Site!

Welcome to the Rudy Giul
Web Site!

Here on this site, you can lea
as Mayor of New York City
principles and values that gav
As New York and the nation
the future. I hope that you wi
opportunity to study the ways
support the other's ideas and

During my watch, New York
one of the biggest cities in the
urban-American center. Jus
that New York was primarily
made New York one of the m
focuses on the world's wealth i
fostered in this respect has he

...upo de artistas-activistas.

ESCAPE ROUTE

Andy

Sam

(like Uncle door!)

bananas

ROLLS

½ mile → café
meet up
right by
bike stop
street
ASAP

chapter one To Salzburg!

As we stumbled off the 8 a.m. train from Vienna, our thrift-store suits felt tight in all the wrong places. It was all we could do to walk without splitting the crotch seams, but the effort kept our minds off our nerves.

"We're here for the CILS conference," Mike croaked as authoritatively as he could to the receptionist at the Crowne Plaza Salzburg.

"Mr. Bichlbauer here is a *speaker*."

"Dr.," Andy corrected.

The woman, puzzled, looked at her agenda.

"Ah! You mean the *conference*. But that starts at ten!"

"We're eager to do very well," Andy said matter-of-factly.

She smiled icily and presented a folder and nametag to Andy. We nodded our thanks, then made our way as calmly as we could to a counter and tore open the folder. We half-expected a "Joke's on You!" in big red clown-letters, just as a squadron of Austrian cops came to take us away. What we found instead was this listing:

International Trade II

Subchair: *Radovan I. Pavelic*, Pavelic & Levitas P.C., Zagreb, Croatia
Moderator: *William Meek*, The John Marshall Law School, Chicago, Illinois, United States.
Speakers:
• *Andreas Bichlbauer*, World Trade Organization, Vienna, Austria. **Trade Regulation Relaxation and Concepts of Incremental Improvement: Governing Perspectives from 1970 to Present.**

From: Wed. 17 May 2000 13: 28:43 EDT
Subject: CILS Confernece, Session on INT'L Trade,
Salzburg, Austria, Oct. 26-29, 2000
: WTO@gatt.org

Mike Moore, Director General, World Trade
Organization (WTO), Geneva, SWITZERLAND

: Conference on International Services, Session
on International Trade, Center for International
Legal Studies, Salzburg, Austria, October 26-29, 2000

Dear Mr. Moore:

I write on behalf of
Director, Center for International Legal Studies
(the CILS"), Salzburg, Austria. More information
about the CILS can be found on the internet at
www.cils.org.

In cooperation with the American Bar Association
section of International Law and Practice and The
John Marshall Law School of Chicago, Illinois,
the CILS is hosting a Conference on International
Services in Salzburg on October 26-29, 2000. A
special session on International Trade is planned.
As subchair of this session, I am looking for four
or five speakers and a panel moderator.

There are usually 60 to 80 participants at these
conferences. Speakers and moderators receive a
substantial discount on accommodation and meals
at the conference's five-star hotel in Salzburg
plus a substantial discount on the conference
fee. Accompanying significant others also receive a
substantial discount on accommodation and meals.

Would you be interested in serving as a speaker at
or as the moderator of the Session on International
Trade? If so, if you would kindly contact me at
the email address as above listed or at my London
chambers' address, telephone, or fax also as above
listed, then I will inform   and he can provide you with more
specific details.

Thank you for your time and consideration.

Sincerely yours,

Moines, New York, London

This was just what we had sent in by e-mail, but we couldn't believe our eyes as we saw it in the official booklet. We hovered as long as we reasonably could, staring at the impossible evidence: we really were in Salzburg, we really had been invited to speak as the WTO, and we really were scheduled to do so in just over an hour.

We really were going to prison!

We made our way to the hotel's breakfast nook, where we drank too much coffee and went over camera operation with Brian, an American friend who had volunteered to videotape the proceedings.

Finally, it was time. At the entrance to our conference hall, an ebulliently obese American pointed us to the moderator, a pleasant-looking lady who was being addressed by an angry man in a 400-thread suit he had clearly *not* found in a thrift store. The subject seemed to be money—something about things going wrong. The lady's passivity and forbearance soothed Andy's nerves, suggesting as it did that she wouldn't ask difficult questions.

Andy approached and confidently stuck out his hand, chivalrously interrupting the angry man in mid-sentence. "I am Andreas Bichlbauer!" he exclaimed to the woman.

24

WE REALLY WERE GOING TO PRISON!

The woman looked confused. "Ah!" said the interrupted man, all his anger suddenly replaced by friendly gusto.

"I'm Bob Hock!" He took the proffered hand and pumped it emphatically. "We need to talk, I need to get information about you. I'm your moderator!"

"Oh! Wonderful!" Andy stammered. "Well! Let's talk!"

Catastrophe already? Andy snuck a pleading look at Brian and Mike.

Mike stepped up and introduced himself. He and Brian were Andy's security detail, he said, "in case anyone attacks him with a pie." Brian's video camera would catch the likeness of a hypothetical pie-thrower, so that same could be prosecuted. "You know how it's been."

Hock nodded in sympathy. "Of course, of course. You come well-monitored." Then, turning back to the hypothetical pie-ee, whose breathing had returned nearly to normal: "Do you have a, you know, short summary, bio…"

Catastrophe two! Of course not, no. We know nothing about Andreas Bichlbauer. There is nothing to say about him besides his name: "I am Andreas Bichlbauer," "This is Andreas Bichlbauer," that sort of thing. What do you think we are, *method actors?*

QUESTIONS —
— DID YOU SEE DR. BICHLZBAUER GET PIED? THEY THREW A PIE AT HIM
↪ DID YOU KNOW HE WAS PIED?
→ DID YOU SEE HIM PRESENT?
→ WHAT HAPPENED?
→ WHAT WERE HIS POSITIONS ON TRADE ISSUES WITH HIS
→ DID YOU AGREE WITH HIS POSITIONS?
→ DID YOU NOTICE ANYONE AROUND
THE HOTEL WHO ACTED LIKE A PROVOCATEUR

→ FOCUS ON BICHLBAUERS

What had we been thinking?

"Something for, you know, my short introduction?" Hock continued, gently trying to soothe Andy's clear discomfiture at the question.

"Well, actually, no... I could write one down for you quickly?" Andy managed.

"That would be wonderful! Obviously I know the name, but I didn't have the moment to look up the credentials."

They made their way to a writing surface, where Hock's energetic kindness rolled on. "I've been teaching WTO—or actually, I've been teaching GATT—for close to 20 years."

"Wow," said Andy, smiling woodenly, his pen poised in air, trying to seem ready to write something down.

"Just to let you know who I am," said Hock, to make this obviously difficult process more manageable for the weirdly fragile Bichlbauer, who lowered his pen in relief, "I'm Professor of Law at John Marshall Law School in Chicago; I've been there for 18 years."

"Wow."

"I founded the international business law center, and the only international economic law masters program in the Midwest."

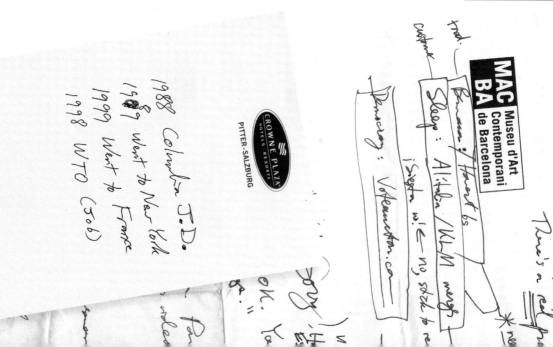

"Wow," Andy repeated, quite sincerely dismayed. "There are about half a dozen in the country."

"Well," Andy finally managed, "I'm afraid my own credentials are not going to quite measure up to yours."

"Nonsense!" Hock said, with the perfect charitable comeback. "I teach what you do."

"Well, all right," said Andy; it came out as a chortle. He began writing: "1988: Columbia. 1989: Went to New York..."

"I just want to make sure I also have your academic credentials," Hock said gingerly over his shoulder.

"Right!" said Andy. "So Columbia University is my alma mater."

"That would be the J.D.?"

"Right! Yes! J..." said Andy, "D...," writing the diploma's initials after the school.

"And you have been with the WTO for...?"

Andy stared up at the ceiling, trying hard to remember. "For the last two years, I've been representing the WTO," he said finally. "And pretty much, my residence is wherever I've been living."

Hock tried to soothe things back to a more reasonable tenor. "Basically, what I'm saying for the panelists' introductions is where they live, where they went to school, their past work, and their area of focus."

"Right," replied Andy, "of course. Of course. Oh!" He pretended to see Mike give him a sign and quickly excused himself, leaving Hock with pretty much none of the above.

Somehow having gotten over the hurdle of being completely unprepared for any conversation whatsoever, we resolved not to converse any more after that. We hovered close together in urgent conference, Andy especially panicking every time Mike or Brian seemed to relax, as if the void might attract conversation. To pass what were possibly our last nervous minutes of freedom, we sketched out our plans for escape. At the first sign of trouble, Mike would move over there, next to the door, clearing the way for Andy and Brian to dash out. Then we would run.

Still needing to fill up some time with officious activity, we determined that *bananas* would significantly enliven the first part of the speech: we authoritatively pillaged the fruit bowl and placed a bunch inside the podium.

As 10 a.m. rolled around, an audience of lawyers slowly made its way in and sat down. The middle-aged men wore smart suits and ties, the lone woman wore a gray mannish suit. At the podium, Bob Hock adjusted the microphone. At the panelists' table, Andy made small talk with the fellow to his left, a Mexican lawyer named Enio Bustamante. Bustamante was originally from the northern reaches of Mexico, Andy learned, but now lived in Mexico City. The North of Mexico was quite humid, sometimes oppressively so. In the winter, though, it never got cold. Never? Never, except in the mountains. The mountains of Mexico? Yes.

WE SKETCHED OUT OUR PLANS FOR ESCAPE.

New York Times, January 5, 2001

Word for Word / Tweaking the W.T.O.

The Long and Winding Cyberhoax: Political Theater on the Web

Finally it was time to begin. Bob Hock made a few general comments of welcome, a brief mention of the morning's subject ("International Trade"), and then, beaming out at the audience, introduced his very special first guest with obvious relish. The interrupted biography had become quite respectable.

"Our first speaker is a distinguished gentleman," Hock intoned: "Mr. Andreas Bichlbauer, of Vienna. He is Austrian by birth, American by training, and Austrian by habitation—so he has come full circle. He got his Juris Doctorate from Columbia University in New York, where he was a *legal scholar*. He has been a representative of the WTO since 1998, speaking on trade matters before a variety of fora, and is one of the authorized voices within the public relations sector of the WTO. Without further ado—Mr. Bichlbauer?"

Stuart Goldenberg

IT'S well known that some regions of cyber-space — Internet chat rooms are one case — are rich sources of misinformation and imaginary characters. But the World Wide Web is also a breeding ground for more elaborate deceptions, as demonstrated by the following cautionary tale about gall and gullibility in the information age.

On Monday early morning, someone at Salzburg, Austria, looks at an official Web site of the World Trade Organization, and the five-year-old Switzerland-based successor to the organization that oversaw the General Agreement on Tariffs and Trade. In Salzburg, Austria, a glance was all they gave it before clicking on the "contact" link and sending a speaking invitation to Mike Moore, the WTO's director-general.

Big mistake: It turns out the site is run by the Yes Men, a loose-knit group of anti-free-trade activists that views hoaxes as a legitimate weapon of protest.

Excerpts of what transpired follow, culled from e-mail correspondence and faxes posted at www.theyesmen.org and:

BARNABY J. FEDER

It didn't take long for the Yes Men to accept the invitation in Mr. Moore's name, even with a caveat.

Thank you for your kind invitation. I may not be able to attend personally, but I would like very much to send a substitute. Would this be possible? Please let me know and I will begin the search process.

Thank you,
Mike Moore

The director of the seminar's sponsor was happy to oblige:

Dear Mr. Moore:

The Nice Project advises me that you wish to send a staff member to speak at the 26-29 October conference in Salzburg.

If you will confirm name of the individual and contact information, I will have further information sent.

Regards, Dennis Campbell
Center for International Legal Studies

At this point, Charles Cushen, a computer programmer in Los Angeles who had been masquerading as Mr. Moore and "Alice Foley," Mr. Moore's secretary, created Andreas Bichlbauer (choosing the name at random from a Salzburg phone book), and made travel arrangements for Dr. Bichlbauer and two "security agents," (including a cameraman). Dr. Bichlbauer raised eyebrows with his speech, titled "Textizen and Consumer as Unit: Trade Regulation and the Free Flow of Incremental Improvement: Governing Perspectives from 1970 to the Present".

Dear Ms. Foley:

We were somewhat puzzled by Dr. Bichlbauer's participation at the conference.

The essential thrust of his argument appeared to be that Italians were a lesser work ethic than the Dutch, that Americans would be better off auctioning their votes in the presidential election to the highest bidder and that the primary role of the U.N. was to serve as a handmaiden to the W.T.O. In the late afternoon, a cameraman (I think it was the same one who filmed Dr. Bichlbauer's speech) appeared at the hotel and sought to interview our delegates. He said Dr. Bichlbauer had been hit in the face with a pie outside the hotel and wanted to know if the delegates thought Dr. Bichlbauer's speech had provoked the attack.

Several of our delegates (including work-ethic impaired Italians) approached me to express concern about the speech, the alleged pie incident

and the cameraman who sought interviews in the late afternoon.

Your clarification will be appreciated.

Regards, Dennis Campbell

Alice Foley's immediate reply:

Indeed you are correct, Dr. Bichlbauer was in fact our representative speaking at the Salzburg C.I.L.S. conference. At present we are not completely certain of all the details, but it appears that our cameraman you mention had something to do with it. Your cameraman seems to do with it. Your cameraman seems to do with it. His cameraman seems to do with it. Our security can never be entirely adequate to the situations we face.

After another message from Mr. Campbell in which he reiterated some delegates found Dr. Bichlbauer's remarks offensive or flippant, the doctor offered his side of the story:

I was disappointed to hear from Alice Foley

that efficiency and the streamlining of culture and politics is at the core of the W.T.O.'s programme, and such practices as described by Dr. Bichlbauer are useful in clarifying the interests of global development as promoted by our organization and others.

On Nov. 1, Alice Foley had more bad news for Professor Campbell:

The situation has, I regret to say, somewhat deteriorated in an already unpleasant state of affairs. Dr. Bichlbauer has contracted a rather serious infection from the pie, which forensic analysis shows contained an active bacillus agent. It is not certain whether foul play was involved.... I know that this question will sound harsh, but could the lawyers present have been angry enough at Dr. Bichlbauer's lecture to do this?

Please, please let us know if anything at the conference struck you as strange, or if you can imagine anyone performing this masterpiece of cowardice, that so threatens to delete Dr. Bichlbauer from our midst in the prime of his usefulness.

On Nov. 6, using addresses collected in Salzburg, Alice Foley e-mailed six conference participants with the message that Dr. Bichlbauer was near death from his infection and concluding:

A similar e-mail message sent two weeks later to 77 delegates elicited a range of responses, most indicating that the result to Italian work habits had been the biggest concern, including "corporate strategy...." The legal center's response on Nov.29 provided the first clear sign that it finally recognized the hoax and asked the Yes Men to "let it rest." Alice Foley issued the following pseudo-clarification to the delegates:

Those who found Dr. Bichlbauer's talk "peculiar," "puzzling" and so on were alert to a situation that has only now become clear to us but overcame a lidized eyes: Dr. Bichlbauer was an impostor! He, his "security guard" and his "cameraman"—belong, it turns out, to an anti-trade cabal called "The Yes Men," who are specifically counter to our own, and who will stop to any level whatsoever to make points. (The point they were attempting to make with this trickery, according to the handwritten letter which we received by this morning's post, had something to do with "corporate anti-democracy," though the syntax and handwriting of the letter are, truth be told, too execrable to make much of.... It is of course extremely embarrassing to us that we can have been conned, like common dowagers, in this way....

Postscript: A W.T.O. spokesman said last week that while his organization deplored the Yes Men's deceptive Web site and the hoax, it respects the nature of the Internet as a forum for free expression. Mr. Cushen said "Mr. Moore" had recently received an invitation to a textile conference in Finland and expects to reply. A reply is required because "the money needed to send a successor to Dr. Bichlbauer. "We think the ethical thing to do is to represent these views honestly than they represent themselves," he said.

Trade Regulation and Concepts of Relaxation and Improvement: Incremental Perspectives Governing from 1790 to Present

This lecture was delivered at the October 27, 2000 Conference in Salzburg, Austria. It was delivered by one International Services since WTO "Andreas Bichlbauer" since not Director-International trade world's available. International of the available. International of the lawyers from some of the attended by largest law firms was accompanied by lecture, which was presentation. a PowerPoint presentation.

Trade Regulation Relaxation and Concepts of Incremental Improvement: Governing Perspectives from 1790 to Present

Trade Regulation
Relaxation from ca. 1970
to the Present

Andreas Bichlbauer
World Trade Organization
5/9/03

Thank you very much. It's a great pleasure to be here, in Salzburg. I'd like to thank the organizers, the other hosts, and everybody who's taken the time to listen, even for a while, to the messages of the WTO.

We'll be talking for the next twenty minutes about impediments to free trade, about the various barriers that have been erected against it over the years—in official, less-official, and completely non-official ways. These barriers, of course, affect not only all of you, but of course all of the world. They are crucial for progress and development and so on and so forth.

Our primary focus to begin with will be on a form of restriction simply called Tariff Trade Barriers. These are ordinary economic impediments to free trade, i.e. tariffs on foreign goods imposed by governments to protect their citizenries against the rational progression of market forces. Everybody knows these, these are the best known.

Some of the others are not as well understood. There are Non-Tariff Trade Barriers, which means anything that is not a tariff but does inhibit trade. This can include legislation—e.g. laws banning the import of tuna caught in nets that kill dolphins, or prohibiting the import of food with carcinogenic pesticide residues, or banning clothes made with slave labor; they can also include ordinary customs and culture, which, like laws, impose arbitrary limits to the functioning of the economy.

32

Finally we have Systemic Trade Barriers, which are the most insidious form of free-trade barrier. These are deep barriers, at the level of systems and structures, at the very core of the governments of most countries today.

In all three cases, we'll be talking not just about problems — there's enough gossip floating around about those already, as I think you all know — but on solutions as well: from past solutions that have worked, or nearly worked, to future solutions that we can only imagine.

Tariff Trade Barriers

Tariff Trade Barriers are what countries have done at various times to isolate their conditions of economic development on behalf of the well-being of their own citizens, or of the citizens of other countries for which they feel some sense of responsibility, for whatever historical reason.

And the most notorious case, that *everyone* associates with trade in many parts of the world, especially among trade-skeptical sectors of the population, is the so-called "honest bananas" case.

You all know the joke: "It isn't possible to kill a person by hitting that person over the head with a banana. It is, however, possible to kill a person over bananas by hitting that person over the head with a machete."

What does this mean?

There's a certain amount of violence in the world — past, present, and future. The EU, in trying to control its bananas, is actually trying to control the violence done in the distant past by European member

Summary
• Tariff Trade Barriers
  Old-style preferences
• Non-Tariff Trade Barriers
  Customs Trade Barriers
• Systemic Trade Barriers
  "Deep" Challenges to a Democratic
  Consumer Society

Europe's Bananas Behavior

states against their former colonies. The EU has done this, however, by paying more for bananas from these colonies than they have to—more, for example, than they would pay for bananas from Central America, produced on much larger farms, using much more modern enforcement techniques.

Yes, violence *has* been committed in Central America on behalf of banana concerns like Dole and Chiquita. Yes, wages *do* average around five dollars per day, with next to no union membership, child labor laws, or worker health standards. But by keeping "violent bananas" out of Europe, the EU is endangering *competition*—and thus the whole edifice of modernity.

When the EU tries to control the bananas of others, the European and US markets both suffer, as does the Central American "political market," if you will. We have an *obsession with violence* interfering with the rational functioning of the marketplace.

Now just to describe this irrational obsession with violence in a little more detail, here are some figures from a study undertaken by Hill and Knowlton of perceptions of violence from 1790 to the present.

In this study, US consumers were asked how much violence they imagined there was in various periods. The chart shows this as "imaginary" violence. For comparison, it also shows *actual* violence—i.e. *violence by people against people resulting in death.*

From 1790 to 1913, as you can see, there's a certain amount of actual violence, on the left, but people imagine a great deal more. Then, from 1913 to 1946, you have two World Wars, a great deal of *actual* violence: it's pretty much off the chart. Yet the

An obsession with violence?

Tariff Trade Restrictions: Considerations, Interpretations

Barriers

34

imagination cannot keep up. Finally, actual violence goes down, yet people still *think* there's a whole lot of violence. In the future, this trend is sure to continue.

Clearly, violence perceptions have nothing to do with violence. For sanity to reign, we must enforce a rational, economics-based approach to violence, an approach in which human emotions can have no place.

Otherwise we are certain to be faced with a situation like in that Jerry Lewis movie, when there's that domino effect—the person slips on the banana. Behind that person is another person, and behind that another—and behind that one a table. On the table, there could well be a computer—perhaps a server maintaining the website of Chiquita. You can see the progression. *Any matter can lead to any other matter.* When the server goes down they lose a day's business receipts, the market value takes a tumble and it takes weeks or even months to recover.

Market Forces, Global Issues

SORRY, I SLIPPED.

To put it more crassly: if we let even one single country pay extra for one single banana, it could open the floodgates—like a wine-drinker becoming a pothead and then graduating to heroin or becoming a coke fiend. When you see your relatives wandering toward you like zombies, you'll sure know you slipped on a banana peel! We must take our bananas seriously.

Trapped

Non-tariff Trade Barriers

Non-tariff trade barriers are a little more complicated. They can include everything from environmental legislation—the dolphin thing—to local customs, which take the place of government in restricting the free flow of goods and money, imposing limits to the proper functioning of economic forces.

Sleep and Failure

Now not long ago KLM, which is based in Holland, and Alitalia, which is Italian, tried to merge. The actual prime variable in this instance was sleep.

In Holland and in most northern countries, you see, people sleep at night, and take at most a small *Mittagsgesundheitschlaf* in the daytime. There's very little distraction from the work environment. There's a fairly regular approach to comings and goings, especially as concerns sleep.

Barriers to Cooperation

In Italy, on the other hand, you have a totally different situation, in which sleep is done during the day as much as at night, almost. Furthermore you have lunches that can last for an hour or two; you can have a nap after that; there's conviviality, hilarity; there's drinking, a little too much wine, there's digging in to *saltimbocca romana* and all of these delightful dishes that end up basically getting in the way of work.

Because of these problems, the merger fails and nothing comes out of it. An opportunity at transnationalism is swept under the rug like so much gold dust.

And this is particularly poignant for us at the WTO, for "alliance" is the WTO's middle name. The WTO sprang out of the GATT, which itself was formed after WWII in an attempt to prevent future wars. The idea — that we still like to communicate — is that patrons rarely kill clients, and those doing business with each other rarely kill one another.

There are exceptions, of course — WWI, WWII, the Rwandan genocide, Yugoslavia, Iraq, etc. But the theory held true in at least one large case — the entire 19th century — when free trade helped to prevent business partners from attacking each other. For 100 years, the sort of trade liberties the WTO enforces today helped maintain peace between the wealthy, powerful countries of Europe, and had an entirely salutary effect, with the sole exceptions of colonialism and the slave trade.

So when mergers are threatened by local peculiarities — when customs impede the forced march of commerce — there's no way to tell what can happen in regards to the full array of transnational interests, and in consequence to the stability of postwar peace.

Local disturbances vs. global alliances
- Hold up production, increase employment overhead
- Fluid dynamics: local irregularities, macro inefficiencies
- Artificial borders to the free flow of capital, always a liability
- The future?

We're faced with a situation in which everything is quite serious. Any artificial impediment to the free flow of capital is a dangerous liability. And what is in the future of this? We don't know. What is the potential solution when not only governments but local variations in culture conspire to impede the free flow of progress?

Mystery.

particu
consu
the g
nece
the
the

in the modern world
Now consumer choi
the democratic pro
and is always ineff
peculiarities that g
manifestation
the
etc. So much vari
inefficiency-whic
democracy.

Fo
se

Summary

ested in the f
to streamli
tem of ele
of a cor
urren

Systemic Trade Barriers

Finally, I'd like to talk about the *most* mysterious, but strangely the most likely to be solved of all three types of trade barriers: Systemic Trade Barriers.

Now we all know what democracy is: it's the participation of the greatest number of consumers possible in the direct functioning of the government and economy. It follows almost necessarily that free trade is the other side of the democracy coin—and thus consumerism is the ultimate form of democracy and citizenry in the modern world.

Now consumer choice is, of course, an essential component of the democratic process—but this role is seldom acknowledged, and is always inefficient. This is because of the vast range of peculiarities that government assumes in today's democracies, the manifestations of popular power: parliaments, congresses, etc. So much variety, so much complexity, can only spell inefficiency—which is sometimes lethal to the idea of a consumer democracy.

Fortunately, we can look to the private sector to see emerging solutions to the vast inefficiencies of so-called democratic institutions.

One possible solution, currently being tested in the field of American politics, is to streamline the grotesquely inefficient system of elections—elections being, of course, at the core of a consumer democracy.

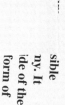

sible
ny. It
ide of the
form of

ent of
dged,
e of
racies,
esses,

sumer

it
s in

ting

tested
quely

l
of

ney

t

Let us first look at elections as they currently unroll, with all their inefficiencies in place.

At the top, we have a number of corporations, let's call them *Corporations A*. From each corporation, involving the work of about 12 employees *per* corporation, goes a great deal of money to a campaign—let's call it *Campaign B*. This can be for any elected official, including the President. From the campaign—involving the work of a great number of workers—goes a great deal of money to a PR agency like Hill & Knowlton—let's call it *C*. From the PR agency, with the help of about 50 employees on full-time salary, goes a great deal of money to TV stations, who, finally, relay the information to the consumer—with *no* transfer of money, of course.

Democracy: Possible paths

And of course the irony of this: in order to generate all the money that it takes to fuel this chain, at the *start* of the chain you have all the workers of the corporations who are also the citizens and the voters at the *end* of the chain. So it's a system that just feeds itself and has very little actual utility.

Now on the other hand, another model: in this case you have the corporations paying, with about the same number of people involved, *one* entity: VoteAuction.com. VoteAuction.com, in turn, employs only four people to transmit not mere information but *actual* money, directly to the consuming voter.

VoteAuction.com is a system that permits voters to voluntarily auction their votes to the highest bidder. It's a forum for people to voluntarily offer their votes for sale, when they don't have a strong affinity for either candidate. It works to streamline the entire process, and as in all market systems, everything works out to the benefit of the consumers—and to the originating corporations, of course.

Summary

So to sum up: we've talked about barriers to free trade past, present, and future. And those barriers that we'd like to see consigned to the past right away are the tariff-based problems—bananas.

Requiring a bit more finesse and a little more care in dealing with people-based opposition is the second type—non-tariff trade barriers, a very important problem in Europe and elsewhere. Different working habits, siestas, etc.: all of this has to be standardized, and this is a very long process.

And finally we have, most complicated of all, systemic trade barriers, which are problems at the core of modern democracies, and yet which *could* be solved by allowing the free functioning of a very competent marketplace. A free marketplace. A *liberated* marketplace. And I like markets, I think this is what markets are for.

Thank you.

if laugh : why did we choose to have the biggest struggle over the [function] thing ?

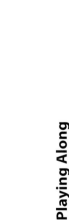

Playing Along

Andy's acting talent is just about nil. His one role in a high school play proved quite disastrous, and in college, after two weeks' rehearsing *The Tempest*, the director wisely ejected him from a bit part before he could ruin the production.

But even without sleep, preparation, or talent, Andy had one essential card that trumped all: the audience came with disbelief pre-suspended. Better, their disbelief had never existed: they *knew* him to be an ordinary WTO representative, and their confidence helped give *him* confidence. By the end of the talk, in spite of himself, he was feeling nearly at one with what he was saying.

The structure of the presentation, progressing in lunacy and unacceptability, had been meant to bring out the maximum reaction in the audience—and to allow Andy to get at least get partway through his speech before being forced from the stage.

The first part, with its bananas and machetes, described a fact on the ground, something already accomplished—in tasteless, horrifying terms, yes, but still real. The next part, about sleep, was grounded directly in current events: in Italy, Berlusconi had already proposed eliminating the siesta nationwide, but had backed off because of public outrage; and in Mexico, the siesta was off-limits in government offices, banned by a new federal policy just six months before.[1]

[1] BBC News, "Siesta gets rude awakening." March 17, 1999.

Andreas Bichlbauer
Austria

The third part of the lecture, however, was incontrovertibly, irremediably insane. Nobody in a position of power would ever propose that corporations be allowed to buy citizens' votes. While it could be said, by a small stretch, to describe the current electoral system in the United States, the phrasing was too outrageous and crude to be plausible. Anyone who had managed to sit quietly through the first two parts of the speech would certainly be helping to wring our necks by the end.

We knew this from experience, for this is just what had happened, on an international scale, to VoteAuction.com just two weeks before.

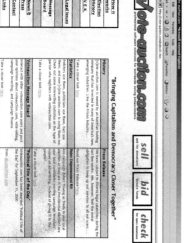

The brainchild of a graduate student named James Baumgartner, VoteAuction.com was an ingenious comment on the way money undermines democracy in the US. At VoteAuction.com, a citizen of California, for example, could put her vote up for auction, then wait for corporate takers. The going price per vote was shown in real

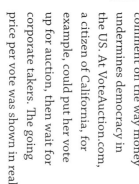

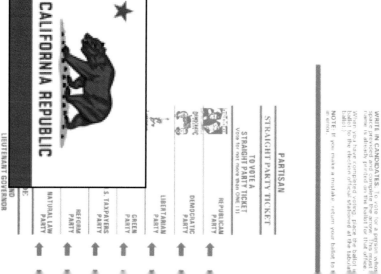

THE PRICE
OF A VOTE IN
CALIFORNIA SEEMED
TO HOVER AROUND
$1—A BARGAIN

time, like on a stock exchange, fluctuating according to the interest of corporations in a particular state. The price of a vote in California seemed to hover around $1—a bargain, the website noted, a small fraction of the amount that corporations currently spent per voter on political advertising in a campaign.

The reaction to VoteAuction.com was swift and nasty. Pundits from Rush Limbaugh to Dr. Laura Schlessinger attacked it. A woman named Deborah Phillips, with a previously unknown group called the "Voting Integrity Project,"[2] became an instant anti-VoteAuction maven and was quoted in most of the coverage. Only two or three journalists seemed to notice that the site was a commentary on the US campaign finance system, which *already* amounts to corporations buying citizens' votes, since corporate contributions drive political campaigns.

Then came the legal threats. The California Secretary of State called the site a "corruption of the voting process" and "one of the most serious political crimes in California and the United States because it strikes at the heart of our democracy."[3] The Chicago Board of Elections filed a lawsuit to stop Chicago residents from being able to buy or sell their

43

[2] The Voting-Integrity.org website has since been taken down.

[3] See www.computeruser.com/ news/00/11/03/news21.html

votes online. In New York, the Board of Elections threatened to have James's thesis advisor, a lawyer, disbarred.

That was enough for James. He turned to ®™ark for help, and Mike and Andy helped him transfer the site to a server in Europe operated by Austrian media artist Hans Bernhard.

But that wasn't the end of it. Two FBI agents showed up at James's door two months later. They were especially concerned about the Austrian connection, as was the Chicago Board of Elections. "We continue to have many investigators out there trying to locate the gentleman responsible in Vienna, Austria and then determine how we might bring him under jurisdiction of the Illinois courts," wrote Langdon Neal, chairman of Chicago's Board of Election Commissioners.[4]

When Andy presented this very same concept to an audience of international trade lawyers in Salzburg, something very strange happened: nothing. While in the real world VoteAuction had triggered FBI raids, among trade lawyers the idea apparently seemed quite sensible. Throughout Andy's description, the audience sat as bored as eunuchs at a strip joint. Bob Hock was the most animated, politely jotting down notes and raising his eyebrows at difficult slides. That was all.

After a nice round of applause. Andy distributed the remaining bananas amid jovial banter, then took his seat to await the vast unknown of the looming Q&A period, a bemused but somehow confident look on his face, and a great deal of confusion in his mind over how he had ever gotten this far.

44

[4] See www.wired.com/news/politics/0,1283,39431,00.html

"HOW DARE THEY SPEAK ABOUT POVERTY AND ALL THE 'GREAT JOBS' THE POOR GET TO HAVE?"

The other panelists' lectures rolled on. Two young Mexico City lawyers talked about the value of the *maquiladoras* to the people of Northern Mexico, while the last panelist de-mystified the art of being a mediator. "A mediator never says no," intoned John V. Sumac, a California mediator who never stopped beaming. "If you create what I call an *indifference curve about language*—if you can find more than one way to acceptably say the same thing—then if you *can't* reach agreement on *one* set of words, *one* phrase, you *can* reach agreement on the other, and *it will mean what the parties need it to mean, and they will have the same meaning.*"

Finally it was time for the questions.

"I'm Peter Rankman, from Washington, and I have a question for Dr. Bichlbauer," a blond, blue-eyed young fellow piped up. He wanted to know what the WTO was doing to educate anti-globalization protesters, who obviously didn't understand the benefits of trade liberalization to the poor—like those "great jobs in Northern Mexico." Clearly the protesters were like he had been in his youth, when he had attended anti-apartheid protests "mostly just to have a good time."

"Indeed," Andy said once the lawyer had finished his three-minute confession, "the protesters *do* tend to have a certain amount of disposable income. They tend to have enough money to travel to protests. They tend to have the *confidence* to travel to protests—without fear of military repression. They must therefore belong to an elite! How *dare* they speak about poverty and all the 'great jobs' the poor get to have?

"To address this irrational and *truculent* young audience, we're working on some extremely active forms of outreach, including *grassroots public relations*, such as is

"ALICE FOLEY"

practiced by various companies. The WTO is so loaded with hatred—uh, the other way around, the *name* of the WTO is so loaded—that you can't really project a friendly image, if you're the WTO, to many sectors of the population. So we're looking to corporations like Philip Morris, with their National Smokers Alliance: we want to perform this kind of *grassroots action, grassroots P.R.*, without identifying ourselves in the equation so much—so as to provide a more *objective* view of our activities unweighted by prior perception."[5]

The next question came from a portly German fellow with a slight speech impediment.

"I'm Heinrich Becker, from Brussels. I wanted to clarify something. You are suggesting that all regional differences must be eliminated in the name of efficiency. Perhaps that is true.

But does it *always* need to happen that way? You can take the EU as example. All trade barriers are eliminated within the EU, but not all regional differences are eliminated. We believe that making everything all the same would make many people quite angry."

"Right!" Andy said. "For that reason we aren't proposing abolishing *all* regional differences. There are many

5 For example, see "The Fake Parade," about a PR company that created an anti-green parade of poor peasants at the Earth Summit in Johannesburg: www.freezerbox.com/ archive/article.asp?id=254. This public relations technique, whereby "corporations create fake "grassroots" organizations to promote their agendas, is commonly called "astroturf." In another instance of "astroturf," Philip Morris hired PR giant Burson-Marsteller to create the National Smokers' Alliance in 1993.

46

Date: Sat, 28 Oct 2000 04:25:28 -0400
From:
To: alice foley <afoley@gatt.org>
Subject: WTO representative

Dear Ms Foley:

We were somewhat puzzled by Dr Bichlbauer's participation at the conference.

He was accompanied by someone we took to be a driver and/or security person and someone who filmed his remarks. The essential thrust of his speech appeared to be that Italians have a lesser work ethic than the Dutch, that Americans would be better off auctioning their votes in the Presidential election to the highest bidder, and that the primary role of the WTO was to create a one-world culture.

In the late afternoon, a cameraman (I think it was the same one who filmed Dr Bichlbauer's speech) appeared at the hotel and sought to interview our delegates. He said Dr Bichlbauer had been hit in the face with a pie outside the hotel and wanted to know if the delegates thought Dr Bichlbauer's speech had provoked the attack.

I have no idea whether or not Dr Bichlbauer was hit with a pie. Certainly there was no public announcement whatsoever that a WTO representative would be with us, and the meeting itself was not open to the public. Nor were the conference schedule or list of participants available to the public.

Several of our delegates (including work-ethic impaired Italians) approached me to express concern about the speech, the alleged pie incident, and the cameraman who sought interviews in the late afternoon.

Your clarification will be appreciated.

Regards,

Center for International Legal Studies

different *languages*, of course, that aren't going to vanish. Different *landscapes*. Different *medical histories*. These things are *facts*—they are not going to change. It's uncertain how much of human reality is biological, but there are *some* things that are mere facts of life.

"But for culture, at least, it's a different story. If you feel that we have not yet reached the point where the flattening of people's cultures leads to general insurrection—and obviously we have not, since there *is* no such insurrection—then we have plenty of room to deal with culture inefficiencies correctly: by eliminating them. At least that's what we feel."

Hock looked at his watch. "At this point I would note that we *are* out of time, and there *is* a luncheon. Lest our other speaker, Mr. Sumac, feel neglected, I will tell him that I was hoping we would get to find out how he would mediate between KLM and Alitalia. Thank you all for your attention; I look forward to seeing you at the rest of the conference."

We followed Peter Rankman, the young lawyer, to lunch. Over food and drinks, we were able to ascertain that he, at least, had really and truly not minded a thing in the lecture.

"The Nazis actually had a reasonable trade policy, you know," Andy found himself saying at one point, to see if Rankman

Date: Sat, 28 Oct 2000 07:01:00-0400
From: Alice Foley <afoley@gatt.org>
To: ████████
Subject: Re: WTO representative

Dear ██

Indeed you are correct, Dr. Bichlbauer was in fact "pied" after speaking at the Salzburg CILS conference. At present we are not completely certain of all the details, but it appears that the cameraman you mention had something to do with it. Dr. Bichlbauer was assigned one official assistant, Ravi Bhaticharaya. Bhaticharaya did not follow proper security protocols in bringing on this cameraman, who seems to have essentially been an agent provocateur who planned the pieing from the start. And we have received one other report linking the "reporter" with this fellow.

I can express our sincere regrets in regards to this matter, and can assure you that Mr. Bhaticharaya's actions will be scrutinized over the next days with the greatest care. We hope you understand that this sort of incident reflects primarily the unfortunate circumstances under which the WTO must accomplish its work, and that our security can never be entirely adequate tothe situations we face.

Please also let me know wheter I may forward your e-mail to parties relevant to the investigation of this matter. And please sned us any more deatils about this incident so that we may pursue our investigation.

As for concerns regarding Dr. Bichlbauer's talk, please be assured that we are certain he did not mean to offend with any remarks. If any parties were indeed offended, please have them write to me with their concerns, and they will be dealt with appropriately.

Best wishes,

Alice Foley
Administrative Assistant to Mike Moore

Totenattentat auf einen WTO-Vertreter? Nein, „Andreas Bichlbauer" wurde in Salzburg nicht getötet. Um auf di[...] kannt zu werden, posierte der US-Hacker aber für den *Falter* mit Schlagobers-Creme im Gesicht / Fotos: Katharin[...]

Der verrückte Professor

CYBER-TERRORISTEN *Für unmerkannter Hochstapler gab sich bei einen privaten Salzburger Rechts-Seminar als WTO-Vertreter aus. Wie er zu der Einladung kam? Die Organisatoren waren auf eine gefälschte Internetseite hereingefallen.*

could be made to mind *anything*. "Maybe they've never really been given proper credit—maybe they're not so bad after all."

"That's not my field of expertise," Rankman replied without hesitation.

"Mine neither," said Andy.

"Are you an economist?" asked one of the Mexican panelists, who had been listening.

"Because economists say that there's no such thing as a free lunch."

"Right," said Andy. "Ha ha. There isn't."

Taking our cue from this dada moment, we put our elegant napkins back on the table and allowed ourselves to finally leave the Crowne Plaza Salzburg.

48

Date: Tue, 21 Nov 2000 18:40:12
To: Delegates: [all seventy-five conference attendees]:
From: Werner Daitz

subject: Conference 2000.10.27

Dear Delegates,

Perhaps you have now heard about the unfortunate event that took place during "Provision of International Services and Sale of Goods" in Salzburg, on the morning of October 27, after Dr. Andreas Bichlbauer's lecture on behalf of the World Trade Organization.

A few hours after that lecture, someone anonymously hurled a pie in Dr. Bichlbauer's face. This would have remained merely another irritating illustration of the WTO's unpopularity in today's world of snap judgments, had Dr. Bichlbauer not contracted a rather severe infection from the pie, which has somewhat spoiled.

We are treating this matter with the utmost gravity, as you can surely understand, and so we are asking everyone who was present at the conference, whether or not you saw Dr. Bichlbauer's lecture, to provide us with the following:

1. If you attended the lecture, we would love to hear your personal reactions to it, as part of our efforts at quality control, and to avoid situations like this in the future. Was the lecture offensive in any way? What struck you the most about it?

2. If you attended the lecture, please convey your impressions of the audience's reaction to it;

please be specific. (If there were any particularly strong reactions, especially from anyone you did not recognize as a delegate, please inform.)

3. Please convey any incidental remarks you may have heard during the conference, regarding the WTO and especially Dr. Bichlbauer's lecture; if you feel comfortable doing so, please attach a name or personal description to each comment.

4. Again as part of quality control efforts, we would appreciate a one-line summary of your opinion of the WTO and its work, and what in particular it might do better in the future. We take your input very seriously.

Thanking you very much in advance,

Werner Daitz.
Public Relations, WTO

Date: Wed. 22 Nov 2000 11:36
From: "████████"
To: "Werner Daitz"
<wdaitz@gatt.org>
Subject: RE: Conference 2000.10.27

The WTO rep. who spoke was the worst speaker at the seminar. His presentation was just plain weird.

The only remarkable "improper" thing he said was when he blamed the Italian poor work ethic as the reason why a merger between KLM and Alitalia could not work out. I did not see the pie incident.

Date: Mon, 27 Nov 2000 18:13:07 -0500
From: Walther Funk <wfunk@gatt.org>
To: CILS conference delegates:
Subject: Unpleasant announcement, URGENT REQUEST

Dear Delegates,

We apologize for interrupting your holiday season with this most unpleasant announcement.

Dr. Andreas Bichlbauer, who spoke on behalf of the WTO at the CILS conference in Salzburg on Oct. 27, and with whom many of you shared a pleasurable moment or two, has passed on. He succumbed yesterday, at 16:50 CET, to an infection thought to have been caught from the rotten pie which was hurled in his face after his Oct. 27 lecture.

We feel sure that you understand the urgency now with which we ask you all to furnish us with any and all information you may have regarding this crime, which to this day remains wholly unsolved. Our only current lead is the "voter fraud" angle. Apparently Dr. Bichlbauer said something in his talk that enraged one of the delegates, so much so that said delegate has refused to speak with us, and has accused the WTO of "encouraging voter fraud."

"Encouraging voter fraud" is furthest from our wishes, of course, and we would like to hear from others who may have heard any statements by Dr. Bichlbauer, that could have been thus misconstrued. Until this subject is resolved we must proceed in the broadest possible manner.

Of course, we do thank those who replied to my colleague Werner Daitz with valuable thoughts and facts, but we are still seeking this crucial bit of information and will appreciate all responses greatly.

A memorial service for Dr. Bichlbauer will take place at the Church of St. Ruprecht at Morzinplatz in Vienna next Sunday at 4 p.m. All those who cannot attend may mail condolences here.

As you can surely understand, we ask that you keep this matter from the press's attention.

Yours until next time,
Walther Funk
Investigative Services

Despite considerable publicity surrounding our Salzburg fiasco, we soon had a second, and then a third, accidental chance to represent the WTO.

The first of these appearances was scheduled for July 19, 2001, one day before 300,000 people were expected to show up in Genoa, Italy, to protest a meeting of the Group of 8, or G-8.

The G-8 are the eight richest countries in the world. Every year or so their leaders get together to dictate world economic policy in a way beneficial to their elites—the richest of the rich. They have no formal basis in international law; their power rests solely on their wealth.

We were expecting big things to happen in Genoa. For the past two years, the anti-corporate movement had been growing rapidly, ever since 40,000 protesters in Seattle had shut down the WTO's Ministerial there. An International Monetary Fund meeting in Prague, and the Free Trade Agreement of the Americas meeting in Quebec, had drawn even more protesters. World leaders found themselves forced to

51

conduct their meetings in fortresses surrounded by seas of angry humanity. Inside the meetings, the leaders of poor countries were starting to stand up and refuse to be bullied into signing agreements they opposed.

Now hundreds of thousands of protestors were expected in Genoa. What would *they* manage to do?

The evening before the Genoa protests were to begin, five hundred miles away in Paris, Andy—or rather, "Granwyth Hulatberi"—entered the French studios of CNBC-TV.

CNBC TV, July 19, 2000

The following is a transcript of CNBC's "European Marketwrap" program, broadcast live on July 19, 2000, the day before the G-8 protests in Genoa. The host was Nigel Roberts, and the guests were WTO spokesperson "Granwyth Hulatberi," Vernon Ellis, International Chairman of Andersen Consulting (renamed "Accenture" shortly before the interview), and Barry Coates, then Director of the World Development Movement (www.wdm.org.uk), an organization that advocates on behalf of poor countries.

NIGEL ROBERTS, HOST: Now tomorrow all eyes will be on the Port of Genoa, where eight of the world's most powerful leaders are gathering for their annual summit, as well as more standard

discussions such as trade, poverty, and so on. The controversial US plan to build a defense shield will also be on the agenda. The man pushing that plan, President George Bush, will be attending the summit for the very first time. So, what can we expect in Genoa?

PRE-RECORDED INTRODUCTION: When eight of the world's most powerful leaders gather in Genoa tomorrow, thousands of protesters will be there to greet them.

Protests are becoming a familiar part of the world's political and economic forums. The starting point was the World Trade Organization's Seattle summit in November 1999, where clashes between the police and protesters put the entire meeting into disarray.

Since then, world leaders have met in battlefield conditions, cordoned off from the public they claim is at the very heart of their policy decisions.

The demographic of the protesters is as wide and varied as the policies that they're protesting about: capitalism, the environment, anti-globalization, and Third World debt unite many against the dominant ruling neoliberal system.

On the eve of the G-8 summit, we asked what are the alternatives for the leaders to consider, what effects protest has on their decision-making, and, if the system has to change, what should replace it. Big questions—there's a lot on

WORLD LEADERS FOUND THEMSELVES FORCED TO CONDUCT THEIR MEETINGS IN FORTRESSES SURROUNDED BY SEAS OF ANGRY HUMANITY.

53

the line, not only economically, but politically and environmentally.

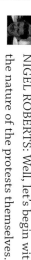 NIGEL ROBERTS: Well, let's begin with the nature of the protests themselves.

Shot divides into four quadrants. Nigel Roberts, Barry Coates, and Vernon Ellis are framed as "talking heads" in generic studio settings; Granwyth Hulatberi is shown in front of the Arc de Triomphe.

We're joined by Vernon Ellis, International Chairman of Accenture; we've got Barry Coates in the studio, he's the director of the World Development Movement; and joining us from Paris, Granwyth Hulatberi [*difficulty pronouncing*], who's a spokesperson for the World Trade Organization.

And really a question for all of you, because let's face it, in the last two years we have seen a tremendous upsurge of anti-capitalist protest. Vern, let me start with you. Why now? What was the catalyst to suddenly get people hitting the streets?

VERNON ELLIS, INTERNATIONAL CHAIRMAN, ANDERSEN CONSULTING / ACCENTURE: Well, I think people hear a lot about globalization, and they feel that somehow there's an *invisible power*.

We at Accenture did a survey of what people in local communities think about multinational corporations. And *I feel they do* believe they *can* do some good.

I personally believe they *can* be good for business—I talked about that last week.

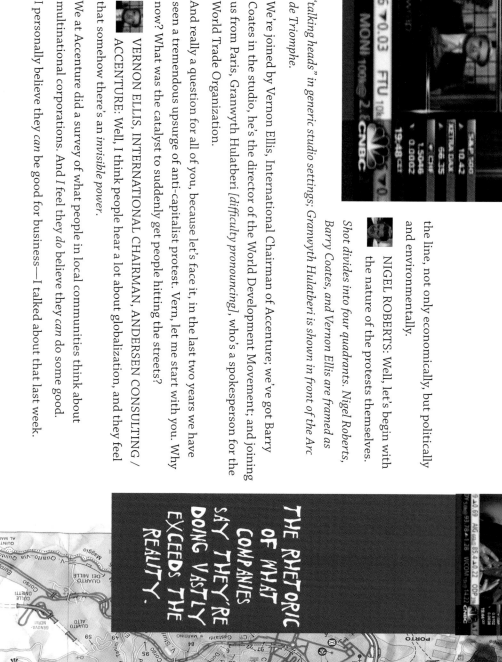

But they also worry that somehow they're remote and unaccountable, and that, I think, gives a sense of unease. Now there's a lot of extreme manifestations of that, but I think that's what's underneath it.

NIGEL ROBERTS: Well Barry, Barry Coates, why is it that there's suddenly been this upsurge?

BARRY COATES, DIRECTOR OF WORLD DEVELOPMENT MOVEMENT: Well, I think two major reasons.

One is that the rhetoric of what companies say they're doing vastly exceeds the reality.

But secondly, and perhaps more importantly in the context of Genoa, is that companies are seen to have undue influence on government policies. And many of the protests around these kind of issues are arguing for change to the rules—to make them fairer to people rather than to create new rights for the big corporations.

I think there's a widespread feeling that governments are too much in the pocket of the corporations. Who suffers from this? It's typically the poor, typically the environment, typically the vulnerable groups in society.

con·sum·er *n.* 1. One that consumes, especially one that acquires goods or services for direct use or ownership rather than for resale or use in production and manufacturing. 2. A heterotrophic organism that ingests other organisms or organic matter in a food chain. (The American Heritage Dictionary, 2000)

BUT WHAT THE PROTESTERS LACK IN THIS ANALYSIS OF THEIRS IS AN UNDERSTANDING

This is still a question of national policy—but it's raised to a new level in the international arena through organizations like the World Trade Organization, the World Bank, and the International Monetary Fund.

NIGEL ROBERTS: Well, Granwyth, you're with the World Trade Organization—perhaps that's a fair point, that more should be being done by organizations like yourself to actually ameliorate those problems.

"GRANWYTH HULATBERI," SPOKESPERSON FOR THE WORLD TRADE ORGANIZATION: Well Nigel, the protesters are of course entirely correct, but we have to see what they're talking about in a relative way.

There is an increase in poverty in the world, there is an increase in inequality, there are various things that the protesters are talking about that are undeniable.

But what the protesters lack in this analysis of theirs is an understanding. I mean you have a mass of protesters, an essentially ragtag group, who are trying to compete with a mass of knowledge that we at the WTO, and experts all over the world, have—knowledge that is based in books that have been written since the 1770s, in England, you know, in the 18th and 19th centuries, about this. These books allow us to be absolutely certain that free trade, although it has led to these problems that the protesters correctly point out, is certain to lead to a bettering of conditions for all consumers.

Shot returns to four-square. Barry Coates' head is cocked to one side in disbelief.

NIGEL ROBERTS: All right, but surely the whole point is that that's what they're protesting about, that in fact it isn't free trade, and that it doesn't actually do what Adam Smith was talking about, which is spreading the greatest

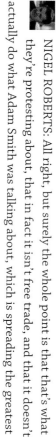

good to the greatest number—it is, actually, divisive: the rich get richer and the poor countries get poorer.

"GRANWYTH HULATBERI": Well, up to the present this is the case. But you bring up poor countries, and we can look at many things that we've been doing to benefit poor countries.

It's sort of a family situation, and families have existed since the Seventh Day, as they say in Jerusalem. You have to look at it that way.

There are "pollution vouchers," which allow countries that want to benefit their economy, I mean their ecology, to benefit it without destroying their economy. We can see ideas such as "justice vouchers," that allow countries which commit heinous human rights violations but want to stop, to stop doing so but in a way that doesn't destroy the social fabric. All of these things.

NIGEL ROBERTS: Barry Coates is dying to come in here, but that in fact just makes the point that's a very contentious issue, global trade. And I think basically what they're saying is that the very idea destroys countries' economies and obliterates individualism.

But of course your boss is a proponent of global trade, Granwyth—Mike Moore, Director-General of the WTO, and this is what he had to say last year in Beijing, why he believes that free trade and globalization is not only important, but essential.

MIKE MOORE, DIRECTOR-GENERAL OF WTO (pre-recorded): Two billion extra souls will share our crowded planet within the next thirty years. We'll have to double food production within about twenty years. We face a world of incredible opportunities and

57

IT'S SORT OF A FAMILY SITUATION. AND FAMILIES HAVE EXISTED SINCE THE SEVENTH DAY, AS THEY SAY IN JERUSALEM.

challenges. Trade and trade policy must play their role as part of a wider development scenario.

NIGEL ROBERTS: All right, Mike Moore there, WTO chief. So, what's wrong with that?

BARRY COATES: It's completely different from the reality of what's going on. Talking about production of food for all—rich countries subsidize their farmers to the tune of twenty thousand US dollars per year, per farmer. Most developing country farmers live on less than *two hundred* dollars per year. And their farming is absolutely destroyed by the dumping of agricultural surpluses on those countries. The supply chains for most of these agricultural commodities are controlled by big corporations.

If the WTO were serious about addressing the issues of world poverty, they would do things completely differently than the way they do now.

NIGEL ROBERTS: An interesting statistic that somebody came out with is to compare the difference between the rich and poor. If you look at the annual global turnover of a firm like Goldman Sachs—I'm not choosing that for any particular reason—$2.2 billion. Look at the GDP of Tanzania: $2.2 billion. The difference is, in Tanzania it's shared out between twenty-five million people; at Goldman Sachs it used to be shared out between 161 partners. Now surely it's that kind of inequality—sure, it might be spreading around, but there's still that divide there.

Let me bring in Granwyth on that. Is that a fair point?

58

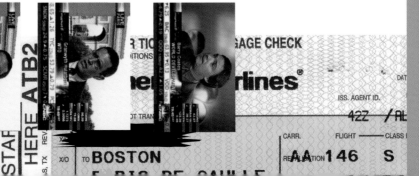

"GRANWYTH HULATBERI": Well, of course it is. But I think Barry, as well as all the other protesters, are simply too focused on reality, and on facts and figures. [Coates shakes his head, his mouth agape.] There's an enormous number of experts at all the greatest universities in the world, who *have* read all these books, who *have* read Adam Smith and everything since it to Milton Friedman, and these people have solid theoretical basis for knowing that things will lead to betterment.

And I think I would have to say that this is a long-term problem that comes down to a problem of education. We have to find a way to convince perhaps not the protesters, but the protesters' children, to follow thinkers like Milton Friedman and Darwin and so on rather than what the protesters have been reared on—Trotsky, and Robespierre, and Abbie Hoffman.

And I think that the direction of education being put into private hands—a concentration of resources in the private sector—will naturally lead to this result, and we'll see the protesters' children being reared with an entirely different set of concerns.

NIGEL ROBERTS: I find very strange the idea that Milton Friedman's a great thinker; the monetarists were let loose in the 1980s, and look what happened then. But let me bring you in on that, Barry.

BARRY COATES: Can I just say that these kinds of simplistic arguments are just too insulting for most people to believe. I mean the idea that we have a choice between Milton Friedman or Abbie Hoffman for where we get our source of economic history and philosophy....

59

There are many, many thinkers from around the world—just not the ones employed by the WTO—that think that World Trade Organization policies are deeply damaging to the development prospects of the poorest countries.

The kinds of policies used by every single OECD country—and by all of the Asian Tigers during their development—are now being closed off by the WTO from use by today's developing countries. As a result, instead of the poorest countries getting richer, what we see is the rising poverty levels of every single region of the world, bar East Asia—and partly because East Asia was able to use policies that helped strengthen their economy, and then they opened up when they were able to compete internationally. What's happening now is that the poorest countries are being opened up too early, when they can't compete, and the domestic industries are being wiped out by well-funded, large foreign competitors.

And there's a very, very solid body of evidence that shows that these gains from trade that the WTO and others talk about have been illusory if you're poor and you live in a poor country.

   NIGEL ROBERTS: Let me go out to Granwyth.
   "GRANWYTH HULATBERI": [*Hulatberi, scribbling notes, is caught by surprise.*] Ah! Yes! Well, I wanted to speak to Granwyth's... sorry, to Barry's point about there being other thinkers.

I'd like to bring up a thinker who's extremely important in our way of thinking, directly as well as indirectly. That would be Darwin, who of course proved that if you look at the natural world, there's one thing you can tell—and that's that things go well.

And so if you take the principles of the natural world and impose them on human society, things will go well too.

And one would have to counter to a statement like Barry's, that there are other thinkers—well, who actually has the power in the world, and therefore who is correct, in this kind of world view? I think the answer is easy. And if you look at the views held by myself, my organization and many, many of the decision-makers in the world—the powerful people—they happen to coincide with what I'm explaining. And I think this is enough, in this sort of view.

BARRY COATES: So what we have here is a

WORLD TRADE ORGANIZATION POLICIES ARE DEEPLY DAMAGING TO THE DEVELOPMENT PROSPECTS OF THE POOREST COUNTRIES.

picture of the rich and powerful people believing a certain philosophy, which they then propound through the institutions in which they have a powerful voice. And I think that this is exactly the model that's being questioned.

Increasingly, there's a large body of people who are concerned about these rules. The people on the streets of Genoa, or of Seattle, are not representative of the overall movement—they are the tip of the iceberg. We did a study last year of developing countries that found that in the space of one year, in fifty protests, more than a million people from developing countries were out trying to change the rules that were being imposed on them by the World Bank and the IMF, and locked in through the World Trade Organization.

NIGEL ROBERTS: Thank you; we must finish up, unfortunately. Barry Coates, thank you very much for joining us, and also Granwyth Hulatbatty (sic), and also Vernon Ellis on the line from New York as well. Quick break; after that we'll wrap up with the markets.

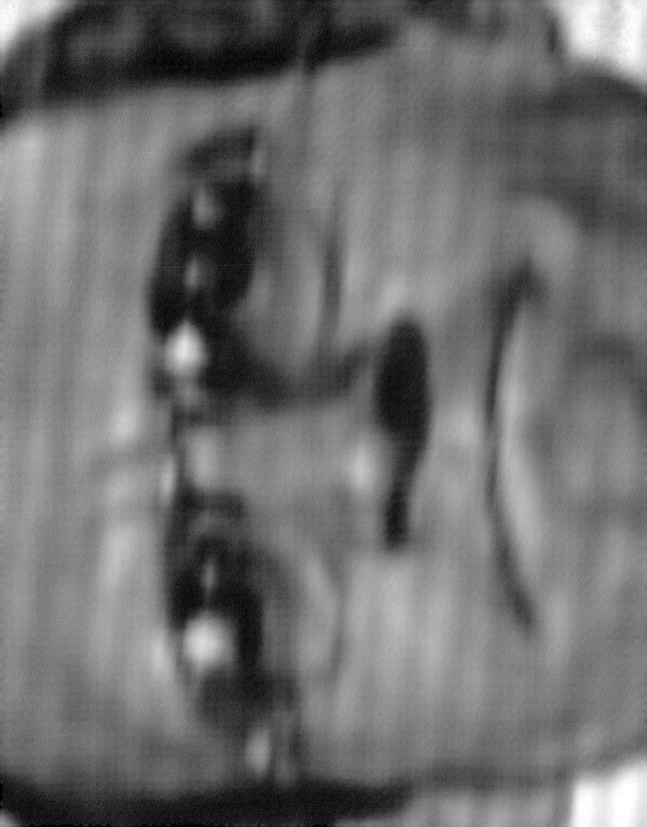

Genoa

Andy left the CNBC studio imagining a platoon of gendarmes waiting for him outside, but found nothing but the cool Parisian night. He made it to the train station just in time for the night train to Genoa, where Mike was already seeing how more conventional protest was faring.

Andy found Mike in a stadium that the protesters were calling home for the week. A quick look around promised that these protests would be anything but conventional. There were samba bands, stilt walkers, and wildly imaginative street theater groups. People in white overalls pushed along huge plastic devices of uncertain use. The "pink bloc" was there, belly-dancing in glittering silver and pink tiaras. Someone was passing out a thousand mirrors in an attempt to recreate the mythical exploits of the Greek mathematician Archimedes, who destroyed invading Roman ships by focusing the reflected energy of the sun. (Actually, that was Mike and Andy passing out the mirrors, but that's another story.) Everywhere was enthusiasm and excitement, and an aesthetic perched precariously between High Medieval and *Romper Room*.

We drove our rental car to the center of Genoa and started looking for parking. Fifteen minutes later, still without parking, we found ourselves in an area where most stores were boarded up.

One hundred yards up ahead was exactly what the storeowners had prepared for: a band of thirty or forty youths in black sweatshirts and balaclavas smashing and torching cars. Suddenly, Andy saw it—our parking spot! He opened his door and called out to a fellow with a large steel pipe in his hand.

"*Scusame!*" Andy yelled, and pointed up to the sign over the parking space. "Okay? *Parcaggio?*"

The fellow stopped, lifted his balaclava, and peered up at the sign. He checked his watch and shrugged. "*Multa*," he said. "You can get a fine."

"But maybe not today, eh?" Andy asked hopefully. "*Oggi?*"

A strange amused look suddenly passed over the fellow's face. He pointed to the band of his comrades burning cars up ahead. As the problem with the location began to register on Andy, another balaclava-clad boy appeared out of nowhere and slammed Andy's door shut. He pointed back up the street. "*Fuori!*" he shouted.

We didn't need a translation. We turned around and drove off the wrong way down the one-way street, thankful we didn't have to worry about getting a fine.

We parked the car and set out on foot. There were violent clashes between protesters and cops in every direction. Sometimes we found ourselves behind police lines mistaken for journalists, then later dodging tear gas canisters fired directly into the crowd. (We were lucky to have brought painters' respirators and diving masks.) Sometimes we were not sure *who* we were with: one group of anarchists turned out to be cops.

By the end of the day, 80 demonstrators had been hospitalized and one, Carlo Giuliani, killed. A somber mood replaced the earlier optimism as news of the death spread around the camps, and wounded people limped back to the stadium to huddle together in the rain.

The next day was the main protest march. Some three hundred thousand people were marching in more conventional groupings. Most were marching with their unions, or, to our surprise, religious organizations calling on the G-8 to erase Third World debt because it was the only moral thing to do. After the mayhem of the previous day, almost everyone was hoping for a peaceful protest.

Suddenly, up ahead, a huge cloud of smoke emerged from the crowd. Near the smoke, people began screaming and running in all directions. A small army of police had blocked off the street, and was firing tear gas directly into the crowd.

Tear gas is incredibly painful when it touches anything sensitive—mouth, throat, nasal passage, or eyes. It makes breathing terribly difficult, and momentarily blinds you if you're not wearing goggles. The pain changed the mood of the crowd completely, as the gas attack turned into a whole series of massive, unprovoked police assaults using weapons ranging from batons to amphibious tanks. Soon bands of unionists were wielding the posts of street

signs as clubs to defend their retreat from marauding cops. Residents threw water bottles down from their windows to help relieve the pain of the tear gas.

Finally the protests came to an end. We were relieved to be leaving the next morning. Fed up with trying to sleep in the stadium among thousands of people—in two days we'd probably managed five hours—we decided to try the beach instead. We checked our e-mail one last time at the nearby Indymedia Center, then drove down the hill to find a spot in the sand. As we descended, we passed a convoy of about twenty police cars and vans going up, the drivers yelling to each other in Italian, fists raised.

An hour and a half later, just as we were about to nod off, word went around that the police had broken into the Indymedia Center and beaten people up. We bolted

awake and raced back up the hill on foot. When we arrived, ambulance workers were carrying stretcher after stretcher out of the school across the street.

The same police we had seen driving up the hill yelling slogans had gone first to the Indymedia Center, from which we had just departed. After smashing a few computers and "confiscating" some videotapes and diskettes, they had gone across the street to the Armando

Diaz school, where several hundred protesters were staying. There they smashed through the doors and, singing fascist songs, bludgeoned a hundred defenseless people bloody, many of them still in their sleeping bags.

The protesters had shattered bones, smashed teeth, fractured skulls. The ambulance workers, presumably seasoned to injury, had ashen looks, and one confided that he thought several of the victims would die. Two nearly did, and 61 required hospitalization, after which most were taken to a police station where, according to all accounts, they were beaten more, humiliated, and forced to sing fascist songs.

We walked silently through the school. There were pools of blood on the ground. Blood soaked out of an empty sleeping bag in which one victim had been beaten. On the walls, bloody streaks traced the routes of victims being hauled downstairs. Three or four people who had managed to hide during the attack were sobbing hysterically. Some other people were leaning out a window, trying to convince someone on the roof that the police were finally gone.

Our last impression of Italy, driving away the next day: small busts of Mussolini for sale in a gas station gift shop.

Back in France, we stopped for dinner at a roadside restaurant. Since leaving Genoa, we hadn't been able to talk about much besides all the terror we'd seen. Now we *had* to focus on something else: our next WTO appearance was just three weeks away in Tampere, Finland, where one "Hank Hardy Unruh" would be the keynote speaker at an international conference called "Textiles for the Future."

We had gone to the law conference in Salzburg, Austria expecting there to be consequences to our actions. We had hoped these would not include extended jail time, or getting our heads smashed in like those of the Genoa protesters, but we had expected *something*.

FIBRES AND TEXTILES FOR THE FUTURE

Hank Hardy Unruh
World Trade Organisation (WTO)
Switzerland

26.3.2004

60th Anniversary of Academic Textile Research and Education in Finland
Fibres and Textiles for the Future
August 16-17, 2001
Tampere, Finland

Thank you for accepting our invitation to give a presentation in the conference. Your presentation's title is:

Future Challenges of Globalisation of Textile Trade

It is scheduled to be presented in the **plenary morning session on August 16**.

If you wish to change the title, please inform us as soon as possible.

We kindly ask you to send us your presentation to be included in the proceedings. The papers shall be submitted to the conference secretariat in electrical form, preferably by **15, 2001**. Please find attached the instructions for submittin...
email: **fibrematerials@tut.fi** as an attachment (rtf-format) to arrive not ...

We kindly ask you to fill in the registration form and ... conference secretariat by fax or by post mail **by June 15** ... lecturer we do not expect you to pay the conference fee... attend the conference dinner on Thursday evening, August ... fee of EUR 70.

Please find attached information on hotels. We recommen... reservation well in advance, because the number of rooms is l... should be paid at check-out directly to the hotel.

Attached, please find the preliminary programme of the conf... will be regularly updated on our website at http://www.tut.fi/units/ms/teva/future/.

Please don't hesitate to contact us if you have something to ask about the conference.
We look forward to seeing you in Tampere in August 2001.

On behalf of the Organizing Committee

Secretary general
Tampere University of Technology
Fibre Materials Science

Thank you for accepting our invitation to give a presentation in the conference. Your presentation's title is: Future Challenges of Globalisation of Textile Trade

Before going on prime time television in Paris, we had been certain that the stream of rubbish we were about to spout would at a minimum prod some producer to pull the plug or broadcast a retraction. Instead, we had been congratulated and promised a copy of the broadcast for our archives.

For this next event, we needed something so completely, incontrovertibly unacceptable that no one could just lap it up without thinking.

Two weeks earlier, we had figured out what that was.

The food arrived. Andy had ordered *tête de veau* because it was the nastiest-sounding thing on the menu, and he wanted something distracting. "Head," the waiter had clarified doubtfully, with a grimace of distaste, clinching Andy's decision.

Before placing the gelatinous mass of assorted head-goop on the table, the waiter held it in front of Andy and wiggled it gently back and forth. It smelled not even remotely familiar—so strange it couldn't even be called repulsive. "You still want it?" the waiter taunted. Andy nodded sadly. The waiter shrugged

Date: Tue, 19 Jun 2001 13:19:58 +0300
From: ▆▆▆▆▆▆▆▆
To: hhunruh@gatt.org
Subject: Attn: Dir. Mr. Unruh: Fibres and Textiles for the Future

Dear Mr. Unruh,

You have accepted our invitation to give a presentation in our Conference Fibres and Textiles for the Future in August (Tampere, Finland). I hope you have received all the relevant material concerning it. I kindly ask you if it is possible for you to send us your paper in advance to be published in the proceedings. For that we would need it by July 15 at the latest. I also ask you to fill the registration form and send it to the conference secretariat as soon as possible to ensure the hotel reservation.

If you have something to ask, please do not hesitate to contact me or the Conference Secretariat (▆▆▆▆▆▆▆▆▆▆▆▆▆▆▆▆▆▆▆). See also the website: http://www.tut.fi/units/ms/teva/future/

With kind regards
▆▆▆▆▆▆▆▆
Tampere University of Technology

...THAT NO ONE COULD JUST LAP IT UP WITHOUT THINKING.

and put it down. "He wants it!" he yelled back to the kitchen, as if settling a bet.

As for Mike's dish, it featured, nestled among a small heap of Brussels sprouts, a single golden sausage half a foot long and three inches thick.

Mike eyed it wistfully. "Well, at least we can look forward to Finland," he said.

Towards the Globalization of Textile Trade

This lecture, presented by "Hank Hardy Unruh," was the keynote address for the "Textiles of the Future" conference held at the

Tampere University of Technology in Tampere, Finland, on August 18-21, 2001. In the audience were one hundred and fifty international research engineers, business people, officials, and academics working in industries ranging from medicine to defense.

Towards the Globalization of Textile Trade

It's an honor to be here in Tampere, addressing the most outstanding textilians in the world today. Looking around at this diverse sea of faces, I see outstanding elements of corporations like Dow, Denkendorf, Lenzing, all at the forefront of consumer satisfaction in textiles. I see members of the European Commission, Euratex, and other important political bodies that aim at easing rules for corporate citizens. I also see professors from great universities walking into a prosperous future hand in hand with industrial partners, using citizen funds to develop great textilic solutions to be sold to consumers for profit and progress.

I see on all of your faces a touching, childlike eagerness to tackle the biggest textiles questions today. At the same time I see a deep understanding that some of these solutions may not be easy, but that come what may, we have to press on into a future that few of us understand, except in terms of its dollar results.

How do we at the WTO fit in? Well, that's easy: we want to help you achieve dollar results. When roadblocks to dollar results arise—protectionism, worry, even violence against physical property—we want to help make sure that none of this stands in the way of your dollar results.

What do we want? A free and open global economy that will best serve corporate owners and stockholders alike. When do we want it? Now.

through now—how we...

What we are doing

Of course, just like nature, the market sorts things out by itself. It's like Darwin said, if you look at nature, one thing is clear, and that's that *things go well*—and that if you apply natural laws to human society, things will go well too.

But like all of us—even wild animals—the market can use some help. And we at the WTO are committed to providing that help, to helping the market help those that need it the most: corporations.

We're using a variety of techniques to do so, all inspired by corporate models. Lobbying, for example. "Guerrilla marketing" to show teenagers the value of liberalization without revealing who we are;[1] and so on.

Finally, we have in mind some far more sophisticated solutions for the future. In just twenty minutes, I'm going to unveil the WTO's own solution to two of the biggest problems for management: maintaining rapport with a distant workforce, and maintaining healthful amounts of leisure. This solution, appropriately enough, is based in textiles.

Workers a problem: how?

But how did workers ever *get* to be a problem? Before unveiling the solution, I'd like to talk a bit about the history of the worker-management problem.

We will follow the stages of work from pre-industrial to an imported workforce model, from an imported workforce to a remote workforce model, and finally—the stage we're going through now—from a remote workforce model to a remote

a
te

O
a 1
a c
dec
of 1
in a

Beli
caus
die a
surp

in thei
textile:

83

---

[1] What Dr. Unruh had in mind was "astroturf," described in footnote 5 of Chapter One.

workforce that *really works*. And incidentally, we'll see that at every step of this evolution, it is textiles that has played the central role.

The first leg of our management-historical journey is back to 1860s America, and the US Civil War. We all know about this war—the bloodiest, least profitable war in the history of the

The US Civil War

US, a war in which unbelievably *huge* amounts of money went right down the drain—and all for textiles!

Of course, this war is most famous for having effected a mighty change in the management paradigm from a central-owner hierarchical model to a much more decentralized, fluid model—a real "hippie revolution" kind of paradigm shift. We'll talk about this misunderstanding in a moment—but first, a bit of background.

Believe it or not, even many *Americans* don't know the *real* causes of the Civil War. Why did people *really* fight and die and lose money? The answer is very simple, but it is surprising. It comes down to one word: *freedom*.

By the 1860s, the South was utterly flush with cash. It had recently benefited from the cotton gin, an invention that took the seeds out of cotton and the South out of its pre-industrial past. Hundreds of thousands of workers, previously unemployed in their countries of origin, were given useful jobs in textiles.

Prosperity

84

Into this rosy picture of freedom and boon stepped...you guessed it: the North.

The North

The South, of course, wanted to buy industrial equipment where it was cheapest, and to sell raw cotton where it fetched the highest price—in Britain. The North, however, decided the South should *not* have the *freedom* to do this, but instead should *have* to do business with the North, and only with the North.

No Excuse for War

The North used its majority stake in the country's governance to exploit the Southern landowners and deny them their freedom to choose the cheapest prices; this of course made them very angry. You'd be angry too if you were denied your freedom of choice! And so the North's abusive tariff practices basically caused what otherwise was a perfectly good market to spiral into a *hideously unprofitable war.*

Civil War responsible for eliminating slavery?

Now *some* Civil-War apologists have stated that the Civil War, for all its faults, at least had the effect of outlawing an Involuntarily Imported Workforce. Now such a labor model is of course a terrible thing; I myself am an abolitionist. But in fact there is no doubt that left to their own devices, markets would have eventually replaced slavery with "cleaner" sources of labor anyhow.

A Thought Experiment

To prove my point, come join me on what Albert Einstein used to call a "thought experiment." Suppose Involuntarily Imported Labor had never been outlawed, that slaves still existed and that it was easy to own one. What do you think it would cost today to profitably maintain a slave—say, here in Tampere?

Let's see.... A Finnish clothing set costs $50 at the very least. Two meals from McDonalds cost $10 or so. The cheapest small room probably runs for $250 per month. For it to function well, you have to pay for your slave's health care—if its country of origin was polluted, this could get very expensive. And of course what with child labor laws, much of the youth market is simply not available.

SLAVE in Finland

Now leave the same slave back at home—let's say, Gabon. In Gabon, $10 pays for two weeks of food, not just one day. $250 pays for *two years of housing*, not a month's. $50 pays for a *lifetime* of budget clothing! Health care is likewise much cheaper. On top of it all, youth can be gainfully employed without restriction.

WORKER in Gabon

The biggest benefit of the remote labor system, though, is to the slave him or herself—because in Gabon, there is no need for the slave not to be free! This is

From Slaves to Workers

86

Now
bett
dece
man.

distan
fashior

Let's lo
out of t
worker
the even
worker |
learn frc
catastrop

in the Sout
Britain's sp
textiles, so

primarily because there are no one-time slave transport costs to recoup, and so the potential losses from fleeing are limited to the slave's rudimentary training. So since the slave can be free, he or she suddenly becomes a worker rather than a slave! Also terrific for morale is that slaves—workers!—have the luxury of remaining in their native habitat and don't have to relocate to places they would be subject to such unpleasantries as homesickness and racism.

I think it is clear from this little thought experiment that if the North and South had simply let the market sort it, they would have quickly given up slavery for something more efficient anyway. By forcing the issue, the North not only committed a terrible injustice against the freedom of the South, but also deprived slavery of its natural development into remote labor.

World Leaders Agree

The WTO is fortunately not alone in understanding the power of the market to resolve serious issues. I quote president George Bush on this matter. At the April 2001 "Summit of the Americas," in Quebec, he said:

"Open trade reinforces the habit of liberty that sustains democracy over the long haul."[2] Had the leaders of the 1860s understood what our leaders understand today, the Civil War would never have happened.

[2] Remarks at the Quebec Summit of the Americas, April 21, 2001 (www.tpa.gov/infodocs/tpa-potus.htm).

Problems with the Remote Labor Model

Now the "modern" remote labor model, while much better than the imported workforce model, is—being decentralized—also much more complicated from a management perspective.

Headquarters

In a world where the headquarters of a company are in New York, Hong Kong or Espoo, and the workers are in Gabon, Rangoon, or Estonia, how does a manager maintain proper rapport with the workers, and how does he or she ensure from a distance that workers perform their work in an ethical fashion?

Let's look at a counterexample, where managers remained out of touch with remote workers, leading to extreme worker dissatisfaction and the eventual total loss of the worker base. Perhaps we can learn from this case and avoid such catastrophes in the future.

Britain

Factories

In 19th-century Britain, just like in the South, things had never looked better. The country was flush with cash, potential, and freedom, thanks to new technology—the spinning jenny. Like the cotton gin in the South—for turning raw cotton into usable cotton—Britain's spinning jenny turned usable cotton into finished textiles, so the British could suddenly mass-produce clothing.

Like in the South, all that was needed was a workforce to produce the raw materials that these new tools required. The British took a modern approach: instead of expensively importing workers as the South had, they located their employment opportunities where workers already lived: India.

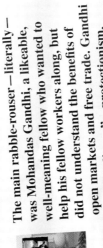

India's resources

There were problems right from the start. For thousands of years India had made the finest cotton garments in the world, so Indian workers felt humiliated providing raw materials to British industry.

A lack of vision

The main rabble-rouser — literally — was Mohandas Gandhi, a likeable, well-meaning fellow who wanted to help his fellow workers along, but did not understand the benefits of open markets and free trade. Gandhi thought that through "self-reliance" — protectionism, really — India could become strong and relearn its own ancient ways of textiles.

These rather naïve ideas became *extremely* popular, and a big proportion of the citizenry rose up against the British management system. *The British eventually had to leave!*

What are the lessons for management here? The big problem in India was clearly a grave lack of management rapport with workers. By making only small adjustments, British management could have kept India on the path to modernity.

Indian textiles

For example, one of the things Gandhi and his anti-globalization followers did was make their own clothing at home, to symbolize their independence from the cotton trade that they perceived as imposed and oppressive. Now as any student can tell you, if management in England had been properly in touch with worker concerns, they could have responded in a timely way—perhaps by making available clothes in the home-spun style that the Indians craved. Today you can see clothes like that in many clothing catalogues, like the *Whole Earth Catalogue*. But of course they didn't have that sort of perspective in Britain and so they couldn't do it.

Undoing Gandhi's mistakes

India still has a long road to recovery from Gandhi's legacy of protectionism. Bill Gates really summed it up on his recent visit to India when he said, "India faces big challenges, such as the existence of well-meaning laws that hinder entrepreneurs. For example, there are laws that say people can't be laid off and that companies can't go bankrupt. As its technological, political, and economic systems are modernized, India's progress will accelerate."[3]

Making Remote Labor Work

Now while the British may be excused for losing India because of a want of technology, we have no such excuse.

[3] www.microsoft.com/billgates/columns/1997q&a/QA970409.asp

In these sensitive times when a large percentage of the world's population is nearing the boiling point over problems they imagine with globalization — when much of the world may be feeling as Gandhi felt, and may be on the point of taking drastic measures — we need to use *all* resources at our disposal to help the market help corporations, to assure that *things go well* — in society just as in nature.

New Solutions

Again, we need to use all the political tools at our disposal, like lobbying. And again, marketing to certain population sectors can change future perceptions. The market, in the form of privatized education, is likely to be our ally in this process of shifting children's awareness from less productive ones, and productive issues and thinkers to more we can help it along as well.

Helping the market sort it out:
Political lobbying

But even more important than any of this is management's on-the-ground efficiency. To avoid another India, we must insure that management is *constantly* in touch with workers, but *constantly*, and not just intellectually — especially the senses. The manager must have direct, visceral access to his or her workers, and must experience their needs in a visceral way.

Staying in touch

but by all the tools at our disposal —

I am now about to show you an actual prototype of the WTO's solution to two major management problems of today. For we all know that not even the best workplace design can help even the most astute manager keep track of his workers. You need a solution that enables *a lot more* rapport with workers—especially when they're remote.

A Solution for Managers

Dr. Unruh steps out from behind podium so he is fully visible to the audience.

Mike, would you please?

Mike follows Dr. Unruh out. In one motion, he grabs the front of Dr. Unruh's suit at the chest and the crotch, gives a mighty yank that nearly pulls Dr. Unruh off his feet, and rips his suit right off. Dr. Unruh's gold lamé body suit is revealed. After regaining his equilibrium, Dr. Unruh raises his arms to the crowd in a gesture of triumph. Applause.

Employee Visualization Appendage

Ah! That's better! *This is the Management Leisure Suit. This is the WTO's answer to the two central management problems of today: how to maintain rapport with distant workers, and how to maintain one's own mental health as a manager with the proper amount of leisure.

I
F:
1

How does the MLS work, besides being very comfortable indeed, as I can assure you it is? Allow me to describe the suit's core features.

Dr. Unruh bends down, grabs a ripcord in his perineal region, and pulls hard. Nothing happens. He tries again. Still nothing. He pulls a second ripcord. This time, there is a violent hissing sound and a meter-long golden phallus inflates forcefully, snapping up and banging Dr. Unruh in the face. Dr. Unruh, now sporting a meter-long golden phallus, turns to the audience and again raises his arms in triumph. More applause.

This is the Employee Visualization Appendage—an instantly deployable hip-mounted device with hands-free operation, which allows the manager to see his employees directly, as well as receive all relevant data about

Leisure

them. Signals communicating exact amounts and quality of physical labor are transmitted to the manager *not* only visually, but directly, through electric channels implanted directly into the manager, in front and behind. The workers, for their part, are fitted with unobtrusive small chips, implanted humanely into the shoulder, that transmit all relevant data directly into the manager.

The MLS truly allows the corporation to be a *corpus*, by permitting total communication within the corporate communication, on a scale never before possible. This is important, but the other, equally important achievement of the MLS has to do with leisure.

Visualizing Employees

MI
rev
do l
are

Now
the
our
not (
to *fe*

Keeping Up

way, s

In the US, leisure—another word for freedom, really—has been decreasing steadily since the 1970s. Compared with 1973, Americans must now work six weeks more per year to achieve the same standard of living.[4] The MLS permits the manager to reverse this trend by letting him do his work anywhere—all locations are equal.

Now the MLS is good for both managers and workers, but the number of non-corporate solutions, also, is as endless as our imagination. For example, with the MLS I'll be able to not only see protests right here on my screen—I'll be able to *feel* them as well. What will the danger level be when the first protester is beheaded? I'm against beheading, but they do that in Qatar, where we're holding our next meeting. The MLS can, in a general sort of way, show us things—it can help us discover new metrics.

Conclusion

This suit—is it a science-fiction scenario? No—*everything* we've been talking about is possible with technologies we have available today.

Keeping Up With The Competition

And even more interesting solutions are being developed. Right here, today and tomorrow, we will be learning about some of the most interesting new solutions from the prime movers themselves.

[4]Juliet Schor, *The Overworked American: The Unexpected Decline of Leisure*, Basic Books, New York, 1992, pp. 79-82.

The very people pioneering these remarkable tools—"living shirts" that monitor a combat soldier's vital signs and motions, for example—will tell us about them in person.

Also here, and of equal interest, are the regulators, trade officials, and others who make the world go round—my colleague Tapio Huuskonen of the European Apparel and Textile Organization, whom I have the pleasure to follow, and my colleague Erkki Liikanen of the European Commission, who will show us tomorrow how traditional industry can be made more useful to the global economy, and who will show us the importance of always looking forward on the highways of progress towards ever new horizons, with cooperation and mutual delight in the fruits of prosperity.

I am *very* excited to be here. Thank you.

In the Cold and Cheerless Northland

Young and aged talked and wondered, well reflected, long debated,
How to live without the moonlight, live without the silver sunshine,
In the cold and cheerless Northland, in the homes of Kalevala.[5]

A Finnish voyage, it turns out, is always fraught with peril, as anyone who has tried to read the collection of folk tales published in *The Kalevala* will know. A tree blocks the sun and moon, and must be chopped down by a finger-sized hero springing forth from the sea; a mother succeeds in reassembling her son from many tiny pieces; because of a golden maiden, a hero must build a boat, but he can't remember the magic words that will allow him to install the boat's "ledges"; a maiden prefers to drown herself rather than marry this hero, and throws herself into the ocean—but the hero then catches her on a hook, for she has become a fish; and so on and so forth, for hundreds of lunatic pages.

Today's traveler is likely to encounter remarkable troubles as well. For example, the clocks in Finland are set one hour ahead of those in most of the rest of Europe.

Perhaps adjusting to time zones cannot be compared to reassembling a hero out of his parts, difficulty-wise. But difficulty is relative, and these are modern times, so when we arrived at the conference center at what we thought was 8:30 am, there was no finger-sized hero waiting to help us. Instead there was only one of the conference organizers, who heaved an

5 All poetry selections in this chapter are from *The Kalevala, or Old Karelian Poems from the Ancient Days of the Finnish People*. *The Kalevala* was put together in the 1830s by a nationalist doctor, Elias Lönnrot, from stories he gathered from Finnish countryside folk.

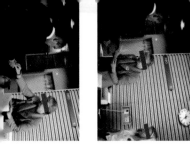

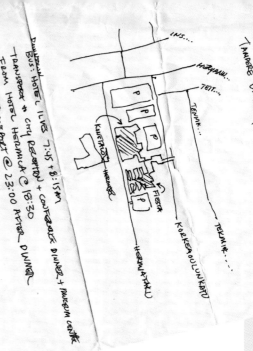

energetic sigh of relief when Andy introduced himself as Dr. Hank Hardy Unruh of the WTO.

"Nice to meet you. We were expecting you." She started frantically assembling Dr. Unruh's conference materials.

Waiting for us? An hour before? We looked at the clock on the wall behind her. The big hand pointed straight down, as expected, but the little hand pointed out to the left and up. "It's not nine-thirty, no, it's eight-thirty, right?" said Andy, pointing.

The woman looked up at the clock, then down at her watch, uttered a "Hmm," and dug around for Unruh's nametag.

"It *is* eight-thirty now, isn't it?" Andy repeated in a somewhat higher pitch.

The woman looked at her watch again and read out the time. "It's *nine*-thirty."

"*Now?*" Andy squealed. "The time is nine-thirty?"

"Yes. Almost. It's twenty-seven past nine, at the moment."

We looked at each other, speechless. "Oh my God," Andy finally managed to gasp. "We start in three minutes."

We started moving towards the lecture hall.

98

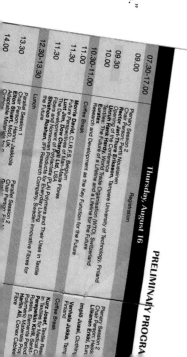

PRELIMINARY PROGRAM

Thursday, August 16

07.30–17.00	Registration	
09.00	Plenary Session 2 Chair Person: Pertti Nousiainen	Plenary Session 2 Chair Person: Heikki Lillanen Erkki, Eur...
09.30	Opening of the Conference Rector Jari-Thure Eriksson	
10.00	Unruh Hank Hardy, World Trade Organisation (WTO), Switzerland Eureka: The Future of Mankind and a Lifetime for the Future	Impö Jussi, Clothing...
10.30–11.00	Coffee Break Research and Development as the Key Function for the Future	Vanhala Jukka, Tampere... Finland
11.00	Morris David, CLRFS, Belgium Future Perspectives of Man-Made Fibres	Coffee Break
11.30	Lunt John, Dow Chargill Ltd, USA The Development of Polylactide (PLA) Polymers and Their Uses in Textile Fibres and Nonwoven Products for Everyday Living	Kurz Josef, Textile Res... in Textiles for Medical Ca...
11.30	Shoo Roshan, IFP Research Company, Sweden Innovative Fibres for the Future	Peräpekki Kirill, Sant-Petersburg Russia... Polymeric Materials Period...
12.30–13.30	Lunch	Herrin Ali, Comex Club...
13.30	Parallel Session 1 Chair Person: Hannu Jaaskola Elton Stuart, MoD, UK Adaptable Materials to...	Coffee Break
14.00	Parallel Session 2 Chair Person: Eric...	

FIBRES AND TEXTILES
FOR THE FUTURE
August 16-17, 2001

Hank Hardy
Unruh
SWITZERLAND

WORLD TRADE ORG.

*On the occasion of
the Conference on Fibres
and Textiles for the Future - 90th Anniversary of
Academic Textile Research and
Education in Finland
the City of Tampere requests the pleasure
of your company at a reception
on Thursday, August 16, 2001
from 19.00 to 20.00
at the Museum Centre Vapriikki*

Vetutiau£o 4

"Are you registered?" the woman asked Mike.

"Um, I'm his assistant," Mike replied.

Our hostess looked at Mike and nodded. "And would you like to join the dinner?" she asked Andy.

"Yes, please." Then Andy had a second thought. "Or is there a fee?"

"No."

"Okay, we'll join the dinner."

The woman grabbed some papers and started towards the conference hall with Andy in tow.

"Um, actually, you can't go in right now," said Mike, grabbing Andy's sleeve. "We have that, ah, urgent phone call...."

Andy froze. The Management Leisure Suit! Andy wasn't wearing it, for it was extremely bulky, and waddling in it all the way from the hotel to the conference

07.30-17.00	
	09.00
Traditional Industry	09.30
gy or Intelligent Clothing?	10.00
nstitute of Electronics,	10.30-11.00
ry New Developments	11.00
s and Design,	11.30
nd Other Oriented	

7

venue had been out of the question. Instead he wore a suit identical to the one designed to cover the MLS; he would change into the real thing on arrival. Andy turned to the woman. "I'm so sorry.... We...have to do something."

"We have to make a phone call," Mike clarified.

"So we'll be just a *tiny, tiny* bit late? I mean later?"

"But your session begins in three minutes?" the woman said.

"Please tell them I'll be three minutes late," Andy said, holding up three fingers. The woman's eyes widened for a moment, then she shook her head and hurried into the conference hall.

We hoped nobody saw us darting together into the restroom next to the telephones. What would they think? That the WTO representative and the WTO representative's assistant both had urgent bladder problems, simultaneously? Or that we were squeezing in some last-second sex as preparation for speaking?

Frantically, Mike pulled the thing out of his bag while Andy stripped down to his underwear. Now the hard part: remembering Sal's instructions, and executing them in a fraction of the time it had taken us when practicing in Paris.

Sal Salamone is a special-effects designer in Hollywood who has a knack for designing the most unlikely costumes. Sal had patiently shown us how to use his insane creation. He had designed it for simplicity, but there's only so simple you can make an inflatable one-meter phallus. Even after three or four test runs, the getting-dressed process required a full 15 minutes of struggle. We'd hoped to give ourselves at least twice that long, hence the early arrival. Now we had less than one tenth the time, and probably ten times the nerves.

"A fucking hour late," said Andy as he tried to jam his foot into the leg. "Wait, wait, shit, go slow," said Mike, as he bent down to untwist the golden fabric. "Fucking time zone... Okay, push."

"One fucking hour," said Andy as he pushed it in and frantically searched for an armhole to fill.

She rakes up half the head, a fore-arm, finds a hand and half the back-bone,
Many other smaller portions; shapes her son from all the fragments,
Shapes anew her Lemminkainen.

After what seemed like an interminable amount of untwisting and filling and zipping and fitting—straps, "EVA," "reservoir," cartridge, second cartridge (backup), breakaway pants, breakaway shirt, breakaway jacket—the Management Leisure Suit and its camouflage over-suit were assembled.

101

WHEN DR. UNRUH WADDLED IN, HUUSKONEN'S EYES LIT UP

Fully reassembled as the manager of the future underneath, but looking exactly like a contemporary manager on the surface, Dr. Hank Hardy Unruh emerged from the restroom together with his security assistant and waddled into the conference hall as fast as he could without breaking his seams.

Two hundred people were waiting. Dr. Tapio Huuskonen, the president of the Tampere University of Technology and primary organizer of the event, was still explaining to the audience that the keynote speaker had encountered a travel adversity of some sort, compounded by a last-minute urgent telephone call, but that he would arrive very soon. When Dr. Unruh waddled in, Huuskonen's eyes lit up—apparently he had gotten to the end of plausible patter.

Now for our second tightrope act. We had planned to hook up the computer to the projector with plenty of time to spare; now we had to do it in front of everyone. Dr. Huuskonen used the opportunity to re-announce that the keynote speaker had arrived, and to explain again who he was. Andy waved to the audience. The audience did not react.

Nor did the computer.

He builds his boat by art of magic, sings a song, and joins the frame-work;
Sings a second, sets the siding—then alas! three words were wanting,
Lost the words of master-magic, how to fasten in the ledges,
How the stern should be completed.

For three minutes, Andy fidgeted with his laptop, under the increasingly icy stares of the audience. Nothing. He tried shaking it gently, then with increasing violence, but it refused to wake from its slumber.

Fortunately this had happened before,[6] and we had prepared a CD backup just in case—but it would take at least 15 minutes to copy the enormous video files depicting the MLS in action to another computer. Mike explained the unfortunate situation to Dr. Huuskonen, apologized and asked to change spots on the program.

Dr. Huuskonen did everything in his power to accommodate the absurd and incompetent team from the WTO. Huuskonen himself would speak first instead of second; the third lecturer would speak second instead of third.

DR. HUUSKONEN DID EVERYTHING IN HIS POWER TO ACCOMMODATE THE ABSURD AND INCOMPETENT TEAM FROM THE WTO.

103

[6] Our piece-of-shit laptop, which never worked very well, was a Sony Vaio XG-9, top of the line.

We set the files to copying over to Dr. Huuskonen's own computer, which he graciously volunteered, and sat down in the audience, thereby concluding one of the most unpleasant 20 minutes of our lives.

Forty minutes later, Dr. Huuskonen took the stage to introduce (again) the fellow who had been billed as the keynote speaker, and was now the *pièce de résistance*.

"Hank Hardy Unruh grew up in Montopolis, Texas, the son of a cattle rancher," Dr. Huuskonen read from the bio. "His early experiences with his father's business imparted to him a lasting interest in trade, and after obtaining his Masters of Business Administration degree, he joined the WTO organization in 1998. Since then he has spoken on trade matters before a variety of fora. He is currently living in Paris."

When a performance is plagued with technical difficulties before it even begins, a forgiving audience will sympathize with the performer, proffering increased attentiveness as a gesture of unshaken confidence in the proceedings. Alternately, they can manifest petulance—remaining passive, stone-faced, a jury set on returning a guilty verdict before the trial has even begun.

Our audience was the latter type—as somber and grim as ancients listening to an eternity of difficult sagas. As Unruh compared slavery with sweatshops and scorned Ghandi as a naive protectionist, he might as well have been reciting all the begats of the *Kalevala*.

Wainamoinen speaks unceasing, speaks the maidens into slumber,
Speaks to sleep the young and aged, all of Northland sleeps.

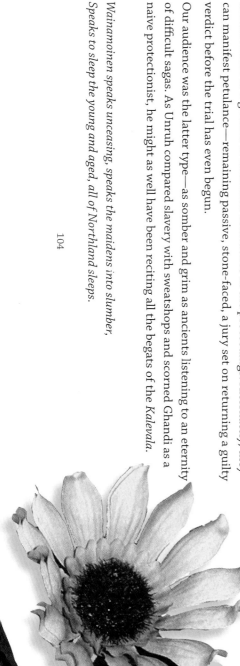

"HANK HARDY UNRUH GREW UP IN MONTOPOLIS, TEXAS, THE SON OF A CATTLE RANCHER"

104

But now it was time for the climax.

"Mike, would you please?"

Andy opened his arms. Mike grabbed the front of Andy's breakaway suit and ripped it off in two hard yanks, revealing Andy in a golden leotard.

Andy raised his fists in triumph. "This," he cried, "is the Management Leisure Suit!"

The audience was suddenly bolt-upright at attention. A gold-lamé suit on the WTO representative? Everything was different now. People clapped and cheered. Excellent! Wonderful! More!

As the Employee Visualization Appendage inflated to its full proportions—the audience was beside itself with excitement.

"THIS," HE CRIED, "IS THE MANAGEMENT LEISURE SUIT!"

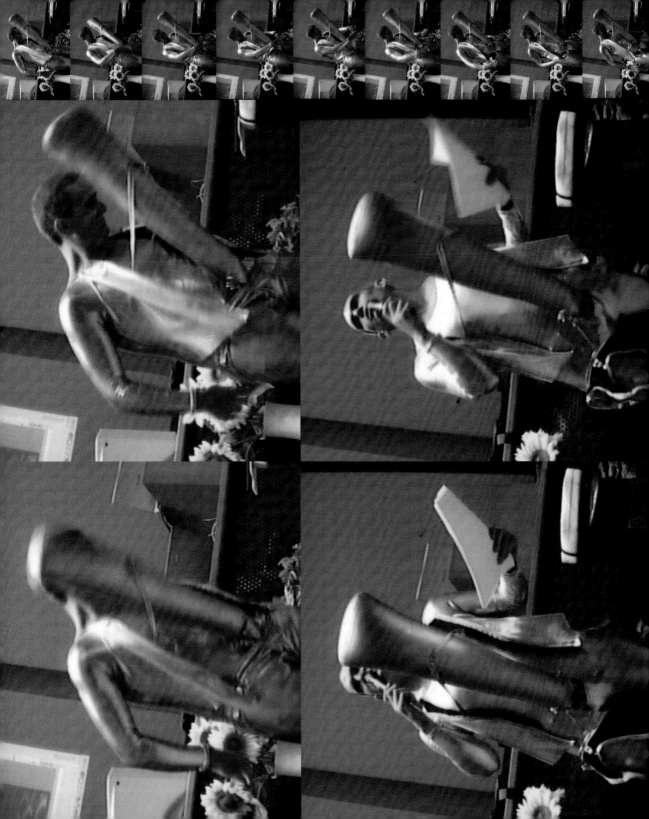

HADN'T ANYONE BEEN OFFENDED?

Out of joy did joy come welling, all of Northland stopped and listened. Every creature in the forest, came to hear his speech of joyance.

The audience was riveted as Dr. Unruh enumerated the uses of his EVA, describing how it would help managers monitor distant factory workers.

At the end, an enthusiastic round of applause. Dr. Huuskonen handed Andy his golden golden underwear, which had somehow fallen off, then asked the audience if there were any questions.

There weren't. The lecture had apparently been self-explanatory. So Dr. Huuskonen asked one himself, a question surely of interest to anyone with textile sweatshops such as those that Unruh had described. What about China? Dr. Huuskonen asked, with reference to its entry into the WTO.

What *about* China, Dr. Unruh replied. Sure China had a dismal human rights record, but we should never consider such things in our trading decisions. And then Dr. Tapio Huuskonen grasped Dr. Unruh's hand and warmly thanked him for his wonderful lecture. The audience offered another round of applause.[7]

As we prepared to follow the audience off to lunch, a young woman with a notepad approached Andy, still in his golden leotard. The local daily, the *Tampere Aamulehti*, had gotten word that a WTO representative was wearing a

108

[7] A week later, informed by a reporter that Dr. Unruh had been a fake, Dr. Huuskonen refused to believe it. "But he was so polite!" he said. "And he had such a very large presentation!"

"WTO representative discusses means of controlling workers via a system of electrical impulsions."

remarkable outfit, and had sent her over to write about it.

In the same detail as during the lecture, Andy explained the uses of the Management Leisure Suit. He even re-inflated the Employee Visualization Appendage for her benefit. Her photographer dutifully took several pictures, and the next morning an article describing the functionality of the WTO's grotesque member appeared in the paper, accompanied by a full-color, half-page photo of the WTO representative with fully erect EVA.

We waddled off to lunch in a cloud of confusion, the air slowly leaking out of the golden member. Where were the cops? The men in white coats with straightjackets? The tomatoes and rotten eggs? We had pulled out all the

llistavat kuidut ja uudet tekniikat
...äävät perinteisen kutomateollisuuden

teollisuus: Esimerkiksi älyvaatteet ja innovatiiviset kuidut ovat tulevaisuuden arkipäivää

109

Bizarre, December 2001

BULLETIN

PRANKS: CULTURE JAMMING
Stunt-troupe jokers, World Trade Center photo hoaxes and the world's tiniest night club

stops this time. We had spent the last three weeks anticipating an extremely dramatic reaction, and nothing but smiles and applause had resulted. Hadn't *anyone* been offended?

Someone must have been. We resolved to find that person, even if it took us from now to the middle of the chilly North-Finland night.

Thou must search for hidden wisdom in the brain of perch and salmon,
In the mouths of ocean whiting, gather wisdom from the cuckoo.

As it happened, it did take us to the middle of the night to find our cuckoo. Meanwhile we spoke to a fellow from Dow ("Interesting lecture!"); a German chemist ("I enjoyed your lecture of course, but only wondered what was its point"); an engineer with a British defense firm ("Your point was obviously that the market would have replaced slavery, given enough time"); and several assorted others who had enjoyed the lecture in various ways. At dinner, Dr. Huuskonen, in his speech to the assembled guests, thanked Dr. Unruh in particular "for showing us the value of always thinking creatively."

After dinner, Andy found himself hobnobbing with the head of the Department of Textiles at Ghent University. "It's the *media* that creates all this protest," the man said in a conspiratorial whisper. "It would be better if you at the WTO could meet and get your work done without notice. But the media needs something to write about, blows it all up, and then suddenly you have all these thousands and thousands of young people there—about nothing!"

110

FHM, January 2002

Action!

L'antimondialisation par la dérision

"About nothing," Andy echoed.

"Nothing!"

"It would be better if the WTO could just meet without anyone noticing," Andy said to make sure he had heard right.

The scientist nodded and handed Andy his card. "You must write to me, I will send you my paper on what should be done with textiles. It is on the desk of everybody in the European Union, this very important paper, and even some in Asia, and you must read it as well, it is a very important paper, it is my view on textiles."

"Yes," said Andy, wondering whether the views it contained just might be as strange as those in the WTO's talk that morning.

A few minutes later we finally met her. *She* had not enjoyed the lecture—so much so, in fact, that at first she refused to tell us why.

"What are you at this conference for?" Mike asked, hoping to get to the subject via another tack.

"I'm here for an intelligent wearables project. Work wear. We're using 'smart' textiles in clothing for work."

"Wow," Andy said. "What does *that* mean?"

"I can't tell you," the woman said. "It's very specific workers we're dealing with."

"Specific?"

"IT'S THE MEDIA THAT CREATES ALL THIS PROTEST."

111

"Well, workers in very hard conditions. Not normal conditions."

"I guess that would be us," Mike said after a pause. "Giving talks like this is very unusual for us."

"Yes," Andy added, "we really have no idea what people think about it. And we want to give many such talks in the future. So we really do want to know…. We'd *love* to know what you think of it."

"Look guys," the woman said. "I'll tell you what was wrong with your presentation. You don't want to hear it, but…"

"Yes we do!" we both said at once.

"Well," she said, "I think your performance was clear. It was brilliant, in fact. I think you showed very nicely how the factory owner needs to be close to the workers. But the way you presented it was not fair."

"Fair?" Andy said.

"It was not fair," she repeated. "You present it as, the males are the owners and the females are the workers. But females can be factory owners too."

Our hearts sank. "Of course," Mike said.

"It's just the…metaphor?" Andy managed.

"Exactly."

"If we changed the… metaphor…." Andy made big circular motions around his chest, as if to show where big golden breasts might be placed.

"Yes," she said. "But don't get me wrong, your performance was brilliant. And you got your point across, that's the main thing."

Mike saw a glimmer of hope. "Can I ask you what that point was, for you?"

"Just the *point*," she said, as if it were obvious. "How to remote-control factories in the Far East, from Europe, the US, wherever—from a different culture."

"So the point was clear," Andy said sadly. "Just the shape was unfortunate."

"A penis is a nice shape," the intelligent wearables expert explained. "I'm only speaking of what it meant."

"What did it mean?" Mike pushed again.

"Male perspective," she said. "Too much."

With the barest of polite excuses, we made our way out to breathe deeply the chilly North-Finland air.

Then the reckless Kaukomieli looked with bended head, ill-humored,
Speaking words of ancient wisdom: "Northland hunters, never, never,
Go defiant to thy forests, in the Hisi vales and mountains,
Like this senseless, reckless hero; I have wrecked my magic snow-shoes."

113

After Finland we were certain that our stint as WTO identity correctors was at an end. The WTO had put a large warning on their web site, warning visitors against our "corrected" site. Furthermore, we were getting even more publicity, in everything from *Fortune* to the *Texas Pagan News*.

Sadly, it seemed we were going out with a whimper instead of a bang. All the press was coming after the fact; our lectures themselves had elicited nothing but applause. We felt like inept puppeteers before incredibly dour children.

Punch kicks Judy: voting must be commercialized and culture eliminated. Punch clobbers Judy: slavery isn't so bad and Gandhi's naïve. Punch KO's Judy: here is a giant golden penis to control distant workers.

The children's reaction: "You are too male-oriented."

Against all odds, another speaking invitation soon arrived, this one from an accountants' association in Sydney, Australia. The subject of their conference was "Business Without Barriers," and they wanted the WTO to come speak on the subject of "Agribusiness Globalization," with special focus on the Australian lamb and Canadian salmon trades.

This time, we swore, the outcome would be different. The event was still months away, leaving us ample time to construct an air-tight, failsafe, 100% devastating portrait of WTO-style globalization that

Will the Real WTO Please Stand Up?

Fortune Magazine, January 2002

115

WE EVEN DECIDED TO DO THE UNTHINKABLE—PRACTICE.

couldn't possibly be misunderstood by anyone. We even decided to do the unthinkable—*practice*. Before a live audience even. Professor Richard Robbins of the State University of New York at Plattsburgh generously reserved an auditorium for a date two months before our Sydney engagement, and promised to publicize our rehearsal as an actual WTO lecture.

For the next four months, from the top of a big round skyscraper outside of Paris, Andy assiduously performed *perruque* ("wig"), the traditional French activity of weaseling time from work to do unprofitable things.[1] For four or five hours each day, he marshaled the resources of mobile-phone giant Cégétel towards the formation of an airtight demonstration of the functioning of the modern market.

The talk grew from five pages to fifteen, then thirty, then settled back down to twelve. The printer ran out of paper many times, out of ink twice. Andy's boss was happy to see him so excited about the company's new accounts and policies, which, like many bosses, he knew nothing about.

While paper, ink, and time were abundant, privacy was not. The concrete stairwell was the only place it could be found, and only for fleeting moments. "Words didn't work, visuals didn't work, so we've got to get right *inside* them," Andy said to Mike.

At the other end of the line in New York, Mike wondered why Andy's voice was echoing so bizarrely.

"*Inside* means *food*," Andy continued. "I'm seeing a hamburger," he

[1] *Perruque* is "the worker's own work disguised as work for his employer. It differs from pilfering in that nothing of material value is stolen. It differs from absenteeism in that the worker is officially on the job. Accused of stealing or turning material to his own ends and using the machines for his own profit, the worker who indulges in *perruque* actually diverts time from the factory for work that is free, creative, and precisely *not* directed towards profit." (Michel de Certeau, *Practice of Everyday Life*)

said even louder. "No, I'm seeing *hundreds* of hamburgers, maybe *thousands*. Sadly, they're all... they're all from McDonald's."

"I see," said Mike.

"And speaking of McDonald's, what else does inside mean, besides food?"

"Privilege?" asked Mike.

"Think *literally*."

"Access?"

Andy thought for a moment. "No. I wouldn't call it access."

"Okay, I give up," Mike said. "What *does* inside mean, besides food?"

Just as Andy was about to answer, Mike heard the sound of a door opening, and the line went suddenly dead.

To our great disappointment, two weeks before our Plattsburgh lecture, the Sydney conference was cancelled. All the meticulous planning we had done for an event halfway around the world was now to culminate in this event a few hours' drive from Mike's house. The "dress rehearsal" had become the main event. We made an extra trip to the thrift store to get just the right shoes for Andy, plus some brown polyester slacks to match the vest Mike had borrowed after a brief stint behind the counter at McDonald's eighteen years before.

New Horizons in Third-World Agribusiness Globalization

This lecture was delivered in March 2002 by "Dr. Kinnahung Sprat', to an audience of three hundred university students at the State University of New York at Plattsburgh.

New Horizons in Third-World Agribusiness Globalization

Hello to all in this wonderful place! I would like to begin by thanking the Economics and Design Schools for inviting us here to impart to their student clientele just a hint of the wealth of knowledge contained in the vast, great field of what we like to call "Business Without Barriers," in all its manifold complexity.

Thanks to all you student clientele, too, for coming with us on our mission. Yes, mission: trade liberalization is, truly, a religious undertaking, a project of faith, a crusade of sorts—and it has been ever since its founders declared that financial success comes from God, that wealth is a sign of divine favor. Today we like to make liberalism sound scientific, and pretend that it's more a matter of fact than of faith, but it's only by remembering the divine nature of our convictions that we can fully maintain them.

I'd like to thank as well our corporate sponsor, McDonald's, who is generously providing the refreshments. Mike Bonanno is passing them out; Mike is Public Relations Officer for McDonald's for the North New York region. Thank you, Mike!

Finally, thanks to the traditional owners of the Plattsburgh region, the aboriginal Mohawks. And today, as it happens, I'm going to unveil an ambitious new plan to help all of the world's downtrodden—yes, including aboriginal New Yorkers!—to integrate more effectively into the global marketplace, conquering excessive hunger while in the process enriching us all.

120

"The poor are the customers of the future..."
General has...
ever so
debilita...
useful m...
investme...

Bear...
I'm g...
prop...
to hel...
real s...
soluti...
unacce...

Why is starvation a problem?

Why is 3rd World
Starvation a Problem?

Now let's start right at the beginning, with the main question: why is Third-World starvation a problem?

First, the facts.

As we all know, investment and exports have been on the rise in the Third World. In 2001, First-World enterprises invested three times more money into Third-World projects than they had ten years earlier. Third-World exports have increased at a similar breakneck pace.

Yet despite this flourishing of trade, there are now 50% more desperately poor people in the world than just 20 years ago! Inequality has doubled in the same period. As a result, almost half the world's population now lives on less than $2 per day.

The cau...

To und...
underst...
today.

In today...
with in h...

Because of the rise in poverty despite increased investment and trade, a growing percentage of people suffer from food-insufficiency diseases like marasmus, kwashiorkor, marasmic kwashiorkor, nutritional dwarfism, etc., whose symptoms include lethargy, inability to work, a host of ailments physical, mental and spiritual, and of course early death. In some places in Africa, for example, fully 80% of the youth population is malnourished in this way!

This kind of situation creates huge problems in the First World. Why? Because every day in which people don't consume food is another day in which they don't participate fully in the global trade that makes us *all* better off.

121

Good news! We managed to convince the Sydney accountants' association to schedule a special luncheon so that the WTO representative could speak after all, despite the cancellation of the big conference.

We mulled over how to incorporate what we had learned in Plattsburgh into our preparations for Sydney. But what *had* we learned in Plattsburgh?

On the one hand, it may be that feeding shit to half the world's population is so outlandish that no one would believe that an official from the organization governing international commerce would ever propose it.

```
-------- Forwarded message --------
Date: Mon, 6 May 2002 06:40:10 +1000
From: ███████████
Subject: Strategic Business Management Conference Sydney - May 21-23, 2002

Dear Mr. Spratt

I am writing to advise that unfortunately on Friday 3 May, CMA Canada and
CPA Australia came to the decision to cancel the above conference. This was
necessitated through the lack of realisation of registrations. I am sorry
to convey this in email to you but I am sure you appreciate the difficulties
in reaching you over the weekend.

I am cognizant of the fact that we have received your paper and will look to
ways and means that this intellectual capital together with the time you
have committed to this event are uti███████
whether we can convert your paper to
Australia magazine, circulation 101,
and revert to you to seek your appro██
```

**"Hildegard Weste" and companion
email the accountants**

149

Dear Hildegarde:

Thank you for your email - I appreciate
your feeling and concern in respect
to the above.   This is just a quick
email to advise that I shall most
certainly endeavour to bring together
people with a like interest to whom
Mr. Spratt may provide say a three quar-
ters of an hour presentation and then
join them for luncheon on 21 May. We
are endeavouring now to put a strategy
into place. I will revert with greater
detail shortly.

In the meantime, would you please advise
Mr Spratt accordingly.

But it is also possible that college *students* are simply
smarter than college *graduates*. That is to say, people
emerge from business school measurably less intelligent
than when they entered. Since the students had begun
reacting as soon as Andy had uttered his first minor
horror, this explanation seemed quite plausible too.

Our intention had been to use Sydney as a laboratory to
test these hypotheses, but in the end, we settled on a new
idea that was so simple, so direct and to-the-point that we
couldn't resist it.

Dear   ;

I am Mr. Sprat's personal secretary, and I am answering
his email while he is away on business. I am dismayed
that the Strategic Business Management Conference is ca-
celled, especially on such short notice.

We are in a somewhat difficult situation, because Mr.
Sprat is already enroute to Sydney for the conference,
with several stops along the way for other meetings and
presentations.

I wonder if there is some way to arrange for him to give

CPA Australia - New South Wales
Tel: (02)
Fax: (02)
Mobile:
Email:

The idea came when Andy showed the tape of the CNBC *Marketwrap* show to Bob. As the tape wound to the end, Bob let out a low whistle. "Nice," he said. *Very* nice. But you didn't go far enough."

"Hunh?" said Andy. "I sounded like a complete imbecile. How could I have gone farther?"

"You could have shut it down," Bob replied.

"Hunh?" Andy repeated.

"Shut it down. Just matter-of-factly announce that you've done an internal review and, Oops! New data! It turns out that globalization really *is* hurting the little guy as the critics are saying, and you're sorry about that, so you're closing it down. They would have had to run retractions all day."

Although not quite prime-time TV, the accounting conference in Sydney seemed like a good enough time to try out Bob's concept. This conference, it seemed certain, would be our last appearance on behalf of the WTO. For whether or not we received any more invitations, we were unlikely to *accept* any more. Life is short, and a year and a half traipsing around the world masquerading as bureaucrats was more than enough.

If our careers as WTO identity correctors were going to come to a close, why not close down the WTO on the way out? It was, after all, the right thing to do.

151

Instead of passing out shitburgers, we would stick to the facts. Lots of them. An avalanche of facts, unleavened by hyperbole, promotion, or hype. Just a simple, systematic explanation of how the WTO steals from the poor and gives to the rich.

And then we would shut it down.

The only problem was, asking us to do something systematically smart was like getting a hedgehog to mow the front lawn. We were used to being funny, abject, and meddlesome; "systematic" and "constructive" were just not in our vocabulary.

We spent the next few weeks trying to fit a square peg in a round hole, until we finally decided to search for outside help. Mike called up Andy in Paris.

"Hey, remember Barry Coates, that really smart guy you were on CNBC with? Did you ever tell him you weren't really with the WTO ?"

"Uh, hmm, no, as a matter of fact."

We took a detour to London before going to Sydney, where Barry Coates worked as the Director of the World Development Movement. We explained to him the truth about Granwyth Hulatberi. Mr. Coates laughed himself into stitches when he realized what we had done, and then generously helped straighten out our tangle of thoughts for the Sydney event.

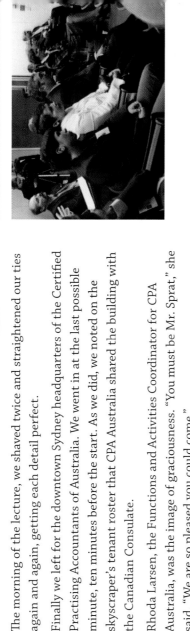

The morning of the lecture, we shaved twice and straightened our ties again and again, getting each detail perfect.

Finally we left for the downtown Sydney headquarters of the Certified Practising Accountants of Australia. We went in at the last possible minute, ten minutes before the start. As we did, we noted on the skyscraper's tenant roster that CPA Australia shared the building with the Canadian Consulate.

Rhoda Larsen, the Functions and Activities Coordinator for CPA Australia, was the image of graciousness. "You must be Mr. Sprat," she said. "We are so pleased you could come."

"Well, it's an honor to say important things to well-meaning people," said Andy somberly, shaking her hand.

"And you must be Mr. Bonanno."

"Mike," said Mike.

"Welcome in any case. Most of our audience has already arrived."

The woman introduced us to several of the functionaries of the association, and to a person who had a peculiar surname: Canadian Consul-General.

"You're really the Consul-General?" Andy asked.

"That's me!" the fellow said good-naturedly.

"Well, thanks for coming!"

"I wouldn't miss it. We need something that really works for our salmon fisheries back home—and of course for the lamb here as well. We do hope the WTO can make decisions that are good for both in the future," he said diplomatically.

Salmon? Lamb? Andy had completely forgotten that the day's topic was supposed to be "Agribusiness Globalization," with a concentration on Canadian salmon and Australian lamb. After learning of this topic six months back, he had downloaded and begun deciphering a host of WTO legal documents about the liberalization of the salmon and lamb trades, in the hopes of finding something interesting to talk about. It was in the midst of this mind-numbing process that Andy had lost interest in luxury foods and decided to concentrate on the other end of the free-market product spectrum: starvation. Hence the hamburgers, now abandoned in favor of Bob's more elegant (and tasteful) solution.

Mike stepped forward.

"I'm with the public-relations office of the WTO," he said. "Mr. Sprat will *not* be talking about salmon and lamb. There's been a change of plans."

"A sudden and *drastic* change of plans," Andy added. "Incredibly drastic. But all-in-all satisfactory."

The Canadian Consul-General looked bewilderedly from one to the other and back again. He began to formulate a question just as Travis Maddington, the "Session Champion," interrupted.

"I think we should get things set up," he said. "It looks like we're ready to start."

WE NEED SOMETHING THAT REALLY WORKS FOR OUR SALMON FISHERIES BACK HOME— AND OF COURSE FOR THE LAMB HERE AS WELL.

THERE'S BEEN A CHANGE OF PLANS.

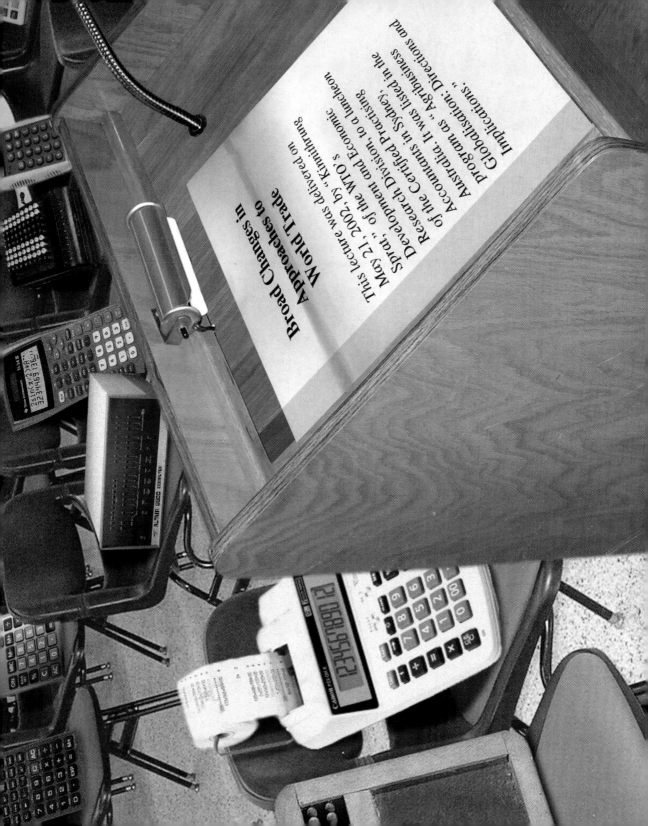

Broad Changes in
Approaches to
World Trade

This lecture was delivered on
May 21, 2002, by "Kinithung
Sprat.," of the WTO's
Development and Economic
Research Division, to a luncheon
of the Certified Practising
Accountants in Sydney,
Australia. It was listed in the
program as "Agribusiness
Globalisation: Directions and
Implications.".

Friends,

I'd like to thank all of you for coming here today, and I'd like to apologize for a rather sudden change in the program, consequent upon a rather dramatic development in Geneva yesterday.

I originally intended to transmit today an upbeat report on the state of world trade. Instead, I find myself the messenger of some rather discomfiting news that affects every one of us in a very profound way, and that augurs a veritable sea-change in our relations with our trading partners, our human-resource constituencies, and within our own organizations. For some of us, this change may be painful.

The news I have just received from Geneva, and that I will be communicating with you today, is not news to those of us who have been at the WTO over the past several months.

As long ago as September, shortly after the events in New York, a rather unprepossessing proposal emerged from a meeting at Lausanne Street, a proposal to make a thorough review of the impact of our work to date, and to lay the groundwork for the leadership we would be called upon to provide in the post-9/11 world.

While most of us present felt that such a reexamination could only be salutary for the organization's vitality, the developments since then have surprised all of us.

158

The organization quickly divided into two camps: those who felt that the charter definitions of the WTO were essentially sound and needed only minor "touching up"; and, on the other side, those who felt that these principles in themselves were *unsound*, and that the organization in its current form was unsalvageable.

I myself sided with the former camp, those who believed reform was desirable and sufficient.

When I first came to the World Trade Organization in 1996, I did so out of a profound belief that the surest path to world peace lay in prosperity, and that the surest path to prosperity lay in the liberation of trade. Was it not true that an entire century nearly free of internecine wars had been characterized by a freedom of trade that has never been equalled? The 19th century's relative peace, I felt, could live once again.

I had *always* felt very strongly—ever since high school, in fact—that a marketplace of free endeavor, liberated from the repressive forces of government regulation, was the way to a happy society. In my high school economics class, I remember watching over the course of the year a ten-part video series in which Milton Friedman expounded the principles of "laissez-faire" economics. I can remember telling my parents they shouldn't lend sugar to the neighbors, since doing so interfered with the market!

My competence at this kind of argument increased greatly at university, where I studied exactly how a marketplace of goods and ideas, maintained through the free play of natural human forces, could bring stability to human society. I became ever more adept at the arguments

upon
leadir
like m
to ortl

showing that when entrepreneurs compete on level playing fields, striving after profit and only after profit, the public benefits, including the poor.

I was at times aware of cracks in this picture, but like the economists I studied with, I felt these to be due to incorrectly applied principles of free trade. Sure, inequality was momentarily growing—but this was a phase through which the world would transition to more equitable distribution through the help of a well-oiled marketplace. Growing poverty, similarly, was a temporary trend that would one day reverse itself. And the entrepreneurial playing field, though dominated by megamergers and an ever more restrained economy that favored the already powerful, would eventually loosen up in accordance with theory.

It was a very considerable psychic distance I had to travel in order to accept that the problems of growing poverty and inequality were not going to simply wither away, that the errors might not be so much temporary glitches as fundamental mistakes in the theory of laissez-faire. But as more and more of my colleagues crossed over into the camp of those who felt that the theory was flawed, and that the WTO in its current form was unsalvageable, I too became overpowered by doubt.

Today, I still believe that the WTO—or at least the GATT—was founded with the poor of the earth in mind, upon the principle that a free marketplace benefits all, leading to prosperity for everyone including the poor. But like my colleagues, I have come to accept that my devotion to orthodox free trade methodologies has betrayed me.

160

This is why I am at peace when I announce to you what I learned yesterday. The WTO will be issuing a public statement by the end of the week, but the die has been cast. As of September 2002, having seen the effects of policies whose only intent was to bring greater prosperity and peace, the World Trade Organization in its present form will cease to exist.

A gasp is heard.

Over the next two years, we of the WTO will endeavor to launch our organization anew along different lines, based on a new understanding of the purposes of world trade. The new organization will have as its foundation and basis the United Nations Charter of Human Rights, which we feel will be a good basis for insuring that the we will have human rather than business interests as our bottom line.

Agreements reached under the WTO will be suspended pending ratification by the new incarnation of our organization, which we are tentatively calling the Trade Regulation Organization.

We are confident that many agreements will be re-ratified in a modified form within the new framework, but there are of course no assurances. I advise all of you who depend upon such agreements to examine them over the next three months with human rights and public prosperity issues in mind.

This news will shock many of you. It still shocks me, even though I have had many months to prepare. These were months in which I learned many things that have profoundly altered my vision of the work that we have

161

On December 10, 1948 the United Nations adopted and proclaimed Declaration Human Rights, the in the following pages. Following Assembly called upon all Member text of the Declaration and "to ca displayed, read and expounded princi educational institutions, without political status of countries or terri

PREAMBLE

Whereas recognition of the inherent and inalienable rights of all member the foundation of freedom, justice a

Whereas disregard and contempt resulted in barbarous acts which has of mankind, and the advent of a wo shall enjoy freedom of speech and fear and want has been proclaimed of the common people,

Whereas it is essential, if man i have recourse, as a last resort, to and oppression, that human rights s ruled by law,

Whereas it is essential to promote th relations between nations,

Whereas the peoples of the United Nations have in the

done, and that have led me to accept that our policies have, overall, had exactly the opposite effect as that which we originally intended.

Understanding the extent of our error has brought me to peace with this difficult decision.

One of the clearest ways to see the extent of our error is to examine the 20 years during which our philosophy has ruled the world, and compare it with the twenty years before that, during which governments had much more oversight over the ways the economy could affect human life.

Between 1960 and 1980, the economies of sub-Saharan Africa grew by 36%. Between 1980 and 2000, their income declined by 15 percent. That's more than a lot of countries lost in the Great Depression!

As for Latin America, its economies grew by 74 percent between 1960 and 1980, but by just *six* percent since then.

The world's 49 poorest countries, which make up 10% of the world's population, have seen their share of world trade decline since 1980 by more than 40%; their share is now at 0.4%.[1]

Around 1.6 billion people are economically worse off today than they were 15 years ago.[2] *Half the world's population* now lives on less than two dollars per day[3]—a figure that has increased by 50% since 1980. Two billion people live with chronic malnutrition, and the number of people living on less than *one dollar per day*—1.3 billion—also seems to be growing in most regions of the world.[4]

income and the p... study has commented: "A new face of... spreading across the globe.... as millions of people live in wretched conditions side-by-side with those who enjoy

since
on aʼ
stag
une
ind

A l
di
th
w

S
1

[1] UNCTAD, Conference on Least Developed Countries 1999, 2001. (www.unctad.org/conference/).

[2] United Nations Human Development Report, 1999, p. 31.

[3] World Bank, Global Economic Outlook 2000.

[4] Ibid.

Even in the wealthiest countries, things have gotten worse since 1980. In the USA, the median income has been stagnating or going down. Today's American must work on average six weeks more per year to achieve the same standard of living as in 1973.[5] There is high structural unemployment in Europe, and there are various other indicators as well that things have gotten steadily worse.

A little perspective helps. On September 11, 3,000 people died in the World Trade Center as a result of terrorism. On the same day, 24,000 people died of hunger, 6,020 children were killed by diarrhea, and 2,700 children were killed by measles.[6]

So who *is* the new regime good for? In simple English, liberalization helps the rich get richer and the poor get poorer.[7]

The gap between rich and poor has doubled in the last 40 years. Today, the richest fifth have 80% of the world's income and the poorest fifth have 1%.[8] As one UNICEF study has commented: "A new face of 'apartheid' is spreading across the globe… as millions of people live in wretched conditions side-by-side with those who enjoy unprecedented prosperity."[9]

Even within the First World, the gap between upper executive and worker salaries has never been bigger—it is in fact many times what it was 20 years ago.[10] Wages of unskilled labor declined by about 25% between 1984 and 1995; unskilled wages in the US have fallen 20% in real terms since the 1970s.[11]

163

[5] Julie Schor, The Overworked American: The Unexpected Decline of Leisure, Basic Books, New York, 1992, pp. 79-82.

[6] New Internationalist Magazine, November 2001. pp. 18-19.

[7] Lundbeg and Squire, World Bank 1999, "Globalization and Inequality: Are They Linked and How?" (www.worldbank.org/poverty/inequal/abstracts/milanov.htm).

[8] United Nations Human Development Report, 1999.

[9] UNICEF figures based on World Bank "World Development Indicators 1997" (www.unicef.org/newsline/pr11.htm).

[10] UNCTAD 1997.

[11] Ibid.

This isn't new, of course. At the start of the 19th century, the ratio of real incomes per head between the world's richest and poorest countries was three to one; by 1900, it was ten to one; by 2000, it has risen to 60 to one ($29,000 to $500),[12] But with trade liberalization of the sort the WTO enforces, the rate at which the rich get richer and the poor get poorer has quickened dramatically.

These are long-range statistics, of course. How about in the short term?

The latest round of trade talks has cost sub-Saharan Africa an estimated US$600 million per year.[13]

UNCTAD estimates that LDCs will lose between $163 and $265 million in export earnings as a result of implementation of Uruguay Round agreements, while paying $146-292 million more for their imports.[14]

This could be why in June 1999, 30 African countries signed a declaration against new trade agreements.[15] This could be why, also, developing nations have used every opportunity—beginning with the Seattle protests—to voice their opposition to WTO trade talks.[16]

Now if the WTO were really serious about reducing world poverty, you'd think it would try to set up trade rules so that whenever possible the poorer countries were at an advantage vis-à-vis rich ones. In fact, however, exactly opposite is the case.

The UN estimates that poor countries lose about US$2 billion per day because of unjust trade rules, many instituted by our organization. This is 14 times the amount they receive in aid.[17]

[12]"The Assessment: The Twentieth Century — Achievements, Failures, Lessons," Angus Maddison, Oxford Review of Economic Policy, winter 1999, cited in Martin Wolf, Financial Times, Jan. 26, 2000 (specials.ft.com/ln/specials/sp57de.htm).

[13]"Africa Recovery", United Nations, 1999 (www.un.org/ecosocdev/geninfo/afrec/vol13no4/30tradbx.htm).

[14]UNCTAD.

[15]"Africa Recovery", United Nations, 1999 (www.un.org/ecosocdev/geninfo/afrec/vol13no4/30tradbx.htm).

[16]UNCTAD, Conference on Least Developed Countries 2001, and World Development Movement, "Briefing from Doha," citing Prof. Alan Winters, "Trade Liberalisation and Poverty," DFID 1999 (www.wdm.org.uk/presrel/current/myths.htm).

[17]The year after this lecture, developing nations would paralyze the WTO and essentially scuttle new agreements during the 2003 Cancún Ministerial.

SEATTLE PROTESTS
SEATTLE

The WTO has consistently allowed First World countries to raise trade barriers protecting their companies, even as we have served as their forum for insisting that Third World countries lower their trade barriers more and more.

Import duties on sugar, for example, are 151% in the US, 176% in Western Europe, 278% in Japan. In Uganda the rate is 25%, and they are being asked to lower it more.[18]

Tariffs on manufactured imports from developing countries are on average four times greater than those on imports from industrial countries. This sort of tariff structure has strongly discouraged Third-World countries from producing high-skill manufactured goods, so their level of development has stagnated.

There are many ways that poor countries are at a disadvantage at the WTO, and hence why they so often get the short end of the stick. One problem is that poor countries have far less access to the WTO decision-making process than wealthier ones.

Only 12 of the 29 least developed countries (LDCs) have offices in Geneva. Many WTO members and observers simply cannot afford a Geneva office. We have approximately 50 meetings per week, and attending them is well beyond the capacity of even those poor countries who *do* manage to maintain an office. What Joseph Stiglitz noted in the case of his organization, the World Bank, holds true for ours as well: "Where developing countries lacked capacity, they were taken to the cleaners."[19]

165

[18]"In Uganda the rate is only 25% and yet we are told to reduce it , and this will affect the 250,000 people involved in sugar in the country. It is a sad story." Ugandan Sugar Producer Mr.M. Mahdevi speaking of striking inequalities in the trade system that make it harder for developing countries to compete; Kampala, August 2001.

[19]UNCTAD launch of the Trade and Development Report 1999.

[20] "African states seek united front on trade," BBC News, Sept. 5, 2001.

[21] Barry Coates, "What's Wrong With Doha," BBC News, Nov. 7, 2002. See also Jeremy Scott-Joynt, "2001 Commonwealth Finance Ministers' Meeting Policy Brief," Commonwealth Studies Institute.

[22] World Bank, "Global Economic Prospectus 2002" (www.worldbank.org/prospects/gep2002/).

[23] UNCTAD Trade and Development Report 1999.

Rich countries tend to corner LDC negotiators in "corridor chats" and offer both promises and threats about aid and investment which many LDCs are ill-equipped to fend off. It is psychologically very difficult to oppose those who are giving you money; the dynamic is that of bribery.[20]

It has now become clear that some LDCs did not realize, when they signed the Uruguay round agreements, what the implications of the agreements would be; the effects of many rules have only become perceptible as they were implemented.

The current agenda of trade negotiations focuses on further opening up markets in the poorest countries, and the extension of WTO rules to investment and services.[21] Most developing countries have proposed instead a focus on making existing trade rules fairer.

According to a World Bank study, eliminating First-World-favoring trade barriers would lift 300 million people out of poverty.[22] UNCTAD estimates that if rich nations opened their markets to LDCs, increased export opportunities would generate an estimated $700 billion of additional trade for the developing world.[23]

Why doesn't this happen?

WTO agreements apply to government policies and actions rather than corporations. This focus dates back to the original thinking behind the Global Agreement on Trade and Tariffs (GATT), signed in 1947. The framers

166

the powerless, and if necessary to use o
despite the long accumulation of momentum that makes

of the GATT — which eventually gave rise to the WTO — perceived their time to be one of powerful states and weak enterprises, and saw the barriers to trade erected by some governments as central to the world's collapse into war.

The situation today is profoundly different. Huge corporations rule the world economy, with much of their activity beyond the regulatory reach of even the strongest and richest states. Yet the WTO continues to address state behavior, leaving corporate behavior unchallenged.

The WTO is used by corporations as a club with which to beat back the few efforts at regulation of their activities that governments have dared to implement. Nearly every single environmental or public health law challenged at the WTO has been ruled illegal. It has been estimated that 80% of America's environmental legislation could be challenged and declared illegal before WTO panels.[24] How can we presume to condemn so sweepingly rules that have been democratically determined?

We cannot. And yet the situation persists. How? Simply put, because that's the way the corporations want it, and they are the ones calling the shots.[25]

I'm sorry that I cannot provide a great deal of detail on the outlines of the new Trade Regulation Organization. This is where the real work begins. In a way, we at the WTO have been experts in the problem; becoming experts in the solution will require a difficult transition.

We do know that the TRO will be founded on the UN

167

it a d
config
road o
into a
for mo

As we
nor ign
have ha
at all.

But as v
let us m
that we
to impro
and for e
tomorrow

Thank yo

[24]Third World Traveller, "World Trade Organization" (www.thirdworldtraveler.com/WTO_MAI/The_WTO.html).

[25]This is a highly abridged version of Mr. Sprat's actual speech, which dragged on for over an hour. For his complete list of statistics, see www.GATT.org/ trastat_e.html.

Universal Declaration of Human Rights, and that the TRO's fundamental goal will be to harness world trade so that it benefits *all* human beings.

All of us must have the heart and courage to find his or her own way of doing something powerful on behalf of the powerless, and if necessary to change our directions, despite the long accumulation of momentum that makes it a difficult move for all of us with a stake in the current configuration. I ask all of you, come join us in this long road of struggle, in this effort to transform world trade into an asset for *all* human beings, rather than a liability for most of them.

As we eat lunch here today, let us not forget the starving, nor ignore the devastating impact that many of our policies have had on the ability of poor populations to eat anything at all.

But as we eat, let us likewise not find a frog in our throat; let us maintain our appetite through the secure knowledge that we have the desire, the ability, and the public support to improve living standards for the poor of the world, and for everyone—through decisions we make today, tomorrow, and far into the future.

Thank you.

168

WORLD TRADE ORGANIZATION

Kinnithrung Sprat
Development and
Economic Research
Counsellor

11 rue De Sie. Marthe
75010 Paris, France
phone: (+33)6-1581-3744
sprat@gatt.org

WORLD TRADE ORGANIZATION

Mike Bonanno
Public Relations
Counsellor

Tour De Alberti
11 rue Sie. Marthe
75010 Paris, France
phone: (+33)6-1581-3744
bonanno@gatt.org

Finally, the Obvious

One hour is a long time to sit through anything without clear plot or punch lines. Yet as Andy droned on with fact after appalling fact, the audience gave him their rapt attention, some periodically nodding in affirmation. When Sprat finally wrapped up, there was a hearty and sincere round of applause.

A shocked Travis Maddington called for questions. At this point it became clear that not only had everyone *believed* the WTO was indeed shutting down, they were *happy* about it. And full of helpful suggestions.

"I'd just like to thank Mr. Sprat for the presentation that he has done here today," Maddington said in closing. "I'm sure it will have a profound effect on the way we and the world do business. We wish you every success, every luck, in the restructuring of what has been an interesting part of world history. Thank you again."

"Thank *you* again," Sprat replied.

Having agreed to the dismantling of the world economy as we know it, everyone went off to eat.

As we moved to the fancy salmon-and-lamb lunch that had been prepared for our visit, we felt none of the nervousness we had felt at previous luncheons. For one thing, there was no ice to be broken; everyone had something real and important to talk about.

It seemed that everyone wanted to tell their own personal story

HAVING AGREED TO THE DISMANTLING OF THE WORLD ECONOMY AS WE KNOW IT, EVERYONE WENT OFF TO EAT.

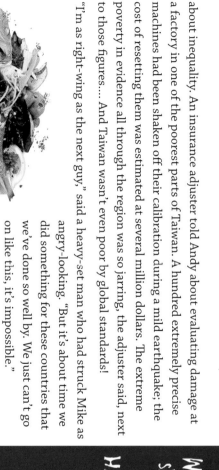

about inequality. An insurance adjuster told Andy about evaluating damage at a factory in one of the poorest parts of Taiwan. A hundred extremely precise machines had been shaken off their calibration during a mild earthquake; the cost of resetting them was estimated at several million dollars. The extreme poverty in evidence all through the region was so jarring, the adjuster said, next to those figures.... And Taiwan wasn't even poor by global standards!

"I'm as right-wing as the next guy," said a heavy-set man who had struck Mike as angry-looking. "But it's about time we did something for these countries that we've done so well by. We just can't go on like this, it's impossible."

One of the officials of the accountants' association offered to draw a logo of the new organization for Andy, and sketched an initial idea on a napkin.

Somebody even produced what ought to have been the winning proposal for a new WTO headquarters. While the real WTO was sifting through ideas for hundred-million-dollar buildings, here we received a proposal that could cost as little as fifty thousand dollars, and that would instantly solve at least one of the WTO's biggest failings: its inaccessibility to its

170

NOT ONLY HAD EVERYONE BELIEVED THE WTO WAS INDEED SHUTTING DOWN, THEY WERE HAPPY ABOUT IT. AND FULL OF HELPFUL SUGGESTIONS.

own poorest members. The concept was extremely simple, and summed up in one line:

Locate the headquarters in a Third-World country.

Forget the design, forget anything else: just build any old building with running water and electricity, but locate it where all WTO members can afford to keep an office: in the poorest place instead of the richest. Developing countries could afford to have more representation in meetings, and First-World delegates would daily witness abject poverty, a constant reminder of the Trade Regulation Organization's new humanitarian bottom line, and of the enormous work that remained to be done.

And so, in the end, one final surprise. One might have thought that there was nothing an audience of international trade experts could do that would surprise us anymore. We no longer assumed we would be thrown off the stage. Nor would we have been caught off-guard if there had been no discussion at all—if everyone had simply filed off to lunch like sheep. What we were entirely unprepared for was everyone being so... *happy.*

"I'M AS RIGHT— WING AS THE NEXT GUY... BUT IT'S ABOUT TIME WE DID SOMETHING FOR THESE COUNTRIES THAT WE'VE DONE SO WELL BY. WE JUST CAN'T GO ON LIKE THIS, IT'S IMPOSSIBLE."

171

My reaction was of one of total surprise. We were expecting a speech more based on what the World Trade Organization does in relation to Australian trade. It sort of blew me out of the water when the announcement was made that the World Trade Organization is significantly reinventing itself to focus on issues relating to people as opposed to economics—something that can hopefully be of significant benefit to the poor and needy throughout the world, in all developing countries.

After all, I think we're all generally aware of increases in poverty and low living standards and other such issues faced by developing countries. And what Mr. Sprat said today really gives a terrific sign of hope for what I think we all aspire to— and that's a global economy that benefits poor people.

WHAT MR. SPRAT SAID TODAY REALLY GIVES A TERRIFIC SIGN OF HOPE FOR WHAT I THINK WE ALL ASPIRE TO—AND THAT'S A GLOBAL ECONOMY THAT BENEFITS POOR PEOPLE.

I WAS ALSO AMAZED TO SEE THERE WAS AN ADMISSION THAT IN FACT IT HAD FAILED.

I thought the speech itself was compelling in terms of its information. I was astounded to find that they're actually going to dismantle the WTO. I was also amazed to see there was an admission that perhaps it had failed. It's going to have a huge effect on international business, and particularly us as an organization.

But the hardest thing, I think, will be with regards to Europe, the E.U. and Japan: will they really change at all in terms of this new organization? Will there be genuine change and real benefits to the poor? It remains to be seen.

I was expecting something on agri-business and what the World Trade Organization does, but I'd have to say I believe it's fairly positive. Because I think that as the gentleman said, the strong are getting stronger and the weak are getting weaker. And you can't let that keep on going. Even we in Australia notice it with some of the trade arrangements that are made: if you're powerful, you can get whatever you like, and if you're not, you lose. And with the world population that we have today, we can't keep going this way.

So I think it was positive. I think it's a very brave decision for an organization to admit that they've been going down the wrong track and to dissolve themselves and to start to look for something different. I think it's fantastic.

SO I THINK IT WAS POSITIVE... I THINK IT'S FANTASTIC.

Our obvious solution to the problem of corporate globalization was obvious to our audience as well. Such joy could not be kept from the world at large, so we sent a press release to 20,000 of our closest friends.

aap MediaNet

Home | company info | product info | media releases | disclaimer

World Trade Centre to Redefine Charter—CPA Australia

WORLD TRADE ORGANIZATION TO REDEFINE CHARTER

At a lunch held today at CPA Australia, Sydney, Kinnithrung Sprat, Development and Economic Research, World Trade Organisation announced the restructure of the World Trade Organisation and the development of the Trade Regulation Organisation.

"After September 30th the World Trade Organisation as we know it will no longer exist," said Mr. Sprat.

The official WTO Media Release follows;

Mr. Sprat is currently at CPA Australia and will be available for comment this afternoon.

WORLD TRADE ORGANISATION
rue de Lausanne 154
CH-1211 Geneva 21
Switzerland

May 21, 2002 For Immediate Release
WORLD TRADE ORGANIZATION TO REDEFINE CHARTER

After a protracted review of current policy, the World Trade Organization will dissolve its current charter and refound under a set of governing principles based in a different understanding of the purposes of world trade. This restructuring was announced today at CPA Australia.

174

The new organization, which pending ratification will be referred to as the Trade Regulation Organization, will have as its basis the United Nations Universal Declaration of Human Rights, with the aim of ensuring that the TRO will have human rather than business interests as its bottom line. The current bilateral agreements system will be replaced with a multilateral system.

The changes come in response to recent studies which indicate strongly that the current free trade rules and policies have increased poverty, pollution, and inequality, and have eroded democratic principles, with a disproportionately large negative effect on the poorest countries.

As of September, agreements reached under the WTO, as well as under GATS, TRIPS, and other frameworks, will be suspended pending ratification by the new Trade Regulation Organization. Many existing agreements are likely to be re-ratified within the TRO, but each one is subject to individual review for ethical qualities within the global picture.

Proposals and resolutions for the foundation of the TRO will be evaluated beginning in June according to their likelihood of furthering the TRO charter. Specifically this will mean redressing the imbalances of existing trade agreements; providing access for developing countries to developed countries' markets; assessing the effects of past trade liberalization and redressing problems where possible; and developing an enforceable framework for special and differential treatment guaranteeing that development policies are not undermined by trade agreements.

Furthermore, principles will aim not only at fixing core problems, but at building a new regime of trust among ourselves (notably between developing and developed members) with civil society organizations (NGOs), and with members of the public. The ultimate aim is to establish rules whose priority is to benefit the poor, improve the environment, and strengthen democratic principles.

A more detailed announcement will be made on Friday, May 24, 2002.

Contacts:
Michael Bonanno, Public Relations, World Trade Organization

Kinnithrung Sprat, Development and Economic Research, World Trade Organization

Kind regards,
CPA Australia New South Wales Division

(Please note new email address & update your records, thank you)
Source: CPA Australia-Original Fax Release

Internet hoax convincing enough to fool Alliance MP

WTO imposter

James Baxter-Southam News

OTTAWA - A Canadian Alliance MP fell victim to an international hoax yesterday that announced the World Trade Organization was closing down and returning as a new organization more sensitive to the needs of developing countries.

The official-looking press release, posted on a Web site run by an anti-globalization group called the Yes Men, appeared so authentic to Alliance trade critic John Duncan that he raised the matter in Question Period.

"Mr. Speaker ... the World Trade Organization has decided to effect a cessation of all operations to be accomplished over the next four months, culminating by the end of September," Mr. Duncan said. "The World Trade Organization will reintegrate as a new trade body, the Trade Regulation Organization. Will the government inform Canadians what impact this will have on our appeals on lumber, agriculture and other ongoing trade disputes?"

Pat O'Brien, parliamentary secretary to Pierre Pettigrew, Minister for International Trade, was understandably confused by the question and offered only a generic response that the government would continue to press its cases before the WTO.

Once made aware of the hoax, Mr. Duncan retracted his comments in the House.

"It was a brilliant master stroke," the somewhat red-faced Alliance MP said later with a chuckle. He complimented the group on its innovative approach and said he only began to suspect the announcement was a hoax as he read the portion that said the organization's head offices would be moved from Geneva to the capital of a less-developed country. Unfortunately, he said, he had only read about half the release when his turn came to ask a question.

"I've certainly learned to be a little more careful when it comes to these sorts of announcements," Mr. Duncan said.

While clearly annoyed, the WTO admitted yesterday that the Yes Men had won the day.

"Some of you may have received a press release from those clever folks at Yes Men, which purports to be a press release from the World Trade Organization public relations," Keith Rockwell, the WTO's director of information and media relations, said in a release of his own. "Needless to say, the communiqué is a hoax.

"While we can appreciate their sense of humour, we would not wish for reputable news organizations like yours to be counted among those duped."

From: <Enquiries@wto.org>
To: "█████████"
Subject: RE: Journalist Inquiry
Date: Mon, 27 May 2002 14:28:32 +0200

Dear Mr. █████

You are refering to the press release from those clever folks at "Yes Men" which purports to be a press release from the "World Trade Organization Public Relations." This press release states that the WTO will disband and be reformed under a new charter as the Trade Regulation Organization. Needless to say, the communique is a hoax. The release is quite cleverly written and it expresses noble sentiments which include addressing the problem of market access for poor countries and the importance of considering the development dimension in trade negotiations. In fact, such sentiments are so noble that the 144 WTO Member Governments committed themselves to precisely these objectives at the Doha Ministerial Conference last November. (http://www.wto.org/english/thewto_e/minist_e/min01_e/mindecl_e.htm) Through the use of their WebSite (www.gatt.org) and other media tools, the Yes Men have had impressive success in duping various organizations around the world into believing that they are representatives of the WTO. While we can appreciate their sense of humour, we would not wish for reputable news organizations like yours to be counted among those duped.

Please contact us if you have any questions.

Information and Media Relations Division
World Trade Organization

-----Original Message-----
From: █████
Sent: 27 May 2002 14:03
To: Enquiries, WTO
Subject: Journalist Inquiry

Greetings-

I am putting together a story for The Toronto Globe and Mail. Late last week a Canadian MP announced in the House of Commons that the WTO was dissolving and being replaced by somthing called the Trade Regulation Organization. I have received a press release from you to that effect. Can you explain more about the process of dissolution? Is there a press release on wto.org about this situation? I am under deadline, so i would appreciate a response as soon as possible.

Thank you,
█████

To: communications@gatt.org

From:
< ████ >

Just a note to commend you all on this
change in policy and your new commitment
to ensuring human rights! The world will
be a better place for this, and you will
have the opportunity to reverse much of
the enormous suffering caused by previous
policies. Thank you for this grand
undertaking.

████ Health & Human Performance
Building
Valley Drive
University of Maryland
College Park, MD 20742

From:
< ████ >

To: <communications@gatt.org>
Subject: WTO release

Wonderful! I am amazed to
see real progress toward
the redistribution of wealth
during my lifetime.

"MR. SPEAKER:
THE WORLD TRADE
ORGANIZATION
HAS DECIDED
TO EFFECT A CESSATION
OF ALL OPERATIONS..."

Dearest ▮

We are very, very sorry that the WTO is not planning to disband this September as previously announced. Others that are sorry include the billions of poor who live on less than $2 per day, and of course "Mother Earth" as the Native Americans might say. We do apologize for the error.

Yours,

Hildegard Weste

To: Hiledgard Weste <weste@gatt.org>

From: ▮▮▮▮▮▮▮▮▮▮▮▮▮▮▮▮▮n>

Subject: Re: WTO to announce schedule for disbanding

Thank you Hildegard for I appreciate your sarcasm grounded in fact.
What I would like to know is why this press release was on www.gatt.org.
Isn't this the official GATT site? Was the press release a "hoax" designed
by social activists to poke at the WTO, and if so, who are they?

Best,

▮▮▮▮▮▮▮

Dear Sir or Madam,

I have not been able to find news in the mainstream US press on the WTO's announcement to disband. I am specifically referring to your Press Release/295, dated 20 May 2002. Please confirm whether this information is true and how I might learn more about it.

Sincerely,

▮▮▮▮▮▮▮▮

New York, USA

Social Entrepreneur

WILL THE GOVERNMENT INFORM CANADIANS WHAT IMPACT THIS WILL HAVE ON OUR APPEALS ON LUMBER, AGRICULTURE AND OTHER ONGOING TRADE DISPUTES?

We live in dark times; laughing is important. We hope you have had some laughs reading about our escapades as WTO spokesmen. Unfortunately, the real-world impact of the policies these clowns are administering is no laughing matter.

Fortunately, there are some very smart people doing very smart work to try to turn this situation around. You won't find them at the WTO, or at the sort of conferences we addressed. You *will* find them in activist organizations spread around the world, working out of cramped offices for little money and with few resources.

They could all use a hand—yours.

Here are some resources to help steer you in the right direction, whether you want to volunteer, make a donation, or educate yourself. The list is not exhaustive; a comprehensive review would fill an entire book in itself, and would quickly become out-of-date, as the movement is very dynamic. What we hope to provide you with here is a way in: get connected with any of these folks, and you will be part of the movement.

Identity Correction, continued

We describe the work of the Yes Men as "identity correction," since our aim is to give a more accurate portrayal of powerful public figures and institutions than they themselves do. These three excellent books offer the perfect counterpart to our public parodies, providing "identity correction" of a deeper sort. Although they may lack the laughs per page of a Yes Men lecture, they have infinitely more substance and detail.

Learning more about the WTO's corrected identity turns out to be a good entry into the subject of international economics, since the WTO has set itself up as both the arbiter of the system and its main pitchman as well. These books will take you from knowing nothing about the subject, to knowing enough to form your own opinions. They will help you understand when and how the corporate hucksters are trying to pull the wool over your eyes, and how to make informed choices about getting involved.

✓ A Citizen's Guide to the World Trade
Organization
By Steven Shyrbam
Published by The Canadian Centre for
Policy Alternatives and James Lorimer
and Co.

✓ The Selling of "Free Trade"
By John R. MacArthur
Published by Hill and Wang

✓ Whose Trade Organization?
Corporate Globalization and the Erosion of
Democracy
Preface by Ralph Nader
By Lori Wallach and Michelle Sforza
Published by Public Citizen

The problem, of course, does not begin and end with the WTO. The WTO is pushing a system which is designed to maximize corporate power and profit. Now, you may think you know how bad corporations really are. But, at least for us, no matter how much we think we know, it always turns out to be worse—and more interesting—than we thought. Fortunately, there is a mountain of good research being done. Our favorite author is Naomi Klein; if you can't read anything else in this section, read these.

✓ *Fences and Windows:*
Dispatches from the Front Lines of the
Globalization Debate
by Naomi Klein
Published by Picador

✓ *No Logo:*
No Space, No Choice, No Job
by Naomi Klein
Published by Picador

For more information: The International Forum on Globalization is an anti-globalization think tank with an online bookstore offering many more excellent titles, including:

Alternatives to Economic Globalization: A Better World is Possible

Fatal Harvest: The Tragedy of Industrial Agriculture

Blue Gold: The Global Water Crisis and the Commodification of the World's Water Supply

and many more. You can find them at www.ifg.org

Act Locally...

Just as the complexities of international trade may seem overwhelming to the average spectator, the possibility of effecting real change may seem far beyond our powers. These matters are supposed to be for "experts" only. We hope the reactions our lectures received show just how hollow these claims of expertise really are, and how important it is that you assume responsibility for your world.

There are thousands of citizens' groups around the globe fighting for human rights and democracy rights and against corporate control. Most do excellent work; some do amazing work. Here are a few that have thought especially hard about ways to help ordinary people play an active role in the movement.

∨ Global Exchange provides an "Act Now" page that offers a list of things that you and your friends can do right away to help people around the world who are fighting corporate power.
www.GlobalExchange.org

∨ Sweatshop Watch is a coalition of both organizations and individuals committed to eliminating the exploitation that occurs in sweatshops. Like Global Exchange, they have gone out of their way to provide ways

for individuals who are unaffiliated with any political group to contribute to the struggle.
www.SweatshopWatch.org

∨ *Earth Action* also provides opportunities for immediate, meaningful involvement, with an emphasis on environmental issues.
www.EarthAction.org

184

✓ *Greenpeace* and *Friends of the Earth* have evolved from small environmental organizations into international organizations fighting corporate power on many fronts. Both of them provide numerous opportunities for direct involvement by citizens.
www.greenpeace.org
www.foe.org

✓ *Global Trade Watch* is a spin-off of Ralph Nader's Public Citizen. Formed in 1995, it tracks US state and corporate policy and behavior in the international arena. The website provides excellent, up-to-date information on US legislation pertaining to globalization, and on how to lobby your representatives on behalf of good policy.
www.citizen.org/trade

... Think Globally

The movement against corporate power is truly worldwide. The World Social Forum, an annual gathering of organizers from around the world, draws some 80,000 participants and 10,000 official delegates (www.wsfindia.org). Of the thousands of organizations those delegates represent, here are just a few of our favorites. In general, these are not organizations that you as an individual can easily join, but knowing the sort of work they do can help you understand the global context of the organizing being done in your area.

✓ The Zapatistas. One of the most sophisticated critiques of globalization has come not from prestigious centers of higher learning, but from indigenous activists in Chiapas. Their influence on anti-globalization activism around the world cannot be overstated.

The official Zapatista web site is www.fzln.org.mx. For those who do not speak Spanish, a good introduction to the Zapatista world is the Mexico Solidarity Network: www.mexicosolidarity.org.

The Third World Network links
organizations fighting the WTO in Africa,
Asia, and Latin America. Based in Penang,
Malaysia, it has additional offices in India,
Uruguay, Ghana, as well as Geneva—also
the home of the WTO—from which
it publishes the daily *South-North
Development Monitor*.
www.twnside.org.sg

Confédération Paysanne. This is the union
of French farmers led by José Bové, who

became a French national hero by using
his tractor to trash a McDonald's.
www.confederationpaysanne.fr

La Via Campesina. José Bové (see above)
has become the international spokesman
for La Via Campesina. Possibly the
broadest coalition of farmers in the
history of the world, La Via Campesina is
fighting to preserve traditional ways of life
in the face of corporate encroachment.
www.viacampesina.org

Steady Your Aim

*These organizations are a few of the many providing specialized help to activists fighting different
aspects of corporate power.*

The Multinational Monitor and
CorpWatch are two organizations that
hold corporations accountable on human
rights, labor and environment issues
through online journalism, education
and activism. If you find your local group
locked in a battle with Engulf and Devour,

Inc., these people can give you inside info
on your adversary that may be extremely
helpful to your cause.
multinationalmonitor.org
www.corpwatch.org

Earth Rights International, a group of lawyers and activists, has been a key player in a series of cutting-edge lawsuits seeking to hold corporations accountable in US courts for abuses abroad: Unocal in Burma, Dow in India, Chevron-Texaco in Ecuador, Shell in Nigeria, etc. www.earthrights.org

Genetic Resources Action International. Efforts by corporations like Monsanto to force genetically-modified, patent-protected seeds on farmers have triggered massive resistance worldwide. GRAIN acts as a clearinghouse for information useful to those engaged in this battle. www.grain.org

Institute for Agriculture and Trade Policy. If you are an independent American farmer trying to hold your own in the face of big agribusiness, these guys can help you understand how US agriculture and trade policies are making your survival

more difficult, and how these policies can be changed. www.iatp.org

Commercial Alert's mission is to "keep the commercial culture within its proper sphere," and in particular to prevent the corporate exploitation of children. They have a health campaign "to reduce the incidence of marketing-related diseases in children," and an education campaign "to rid the nation's schools of corporate marketers, junk food peddlers and market researchers, and to banish their influence upon textbooks and curricula as well." www.commercialalert.org

The Real Deal

Finally, you might want to go back to the source.

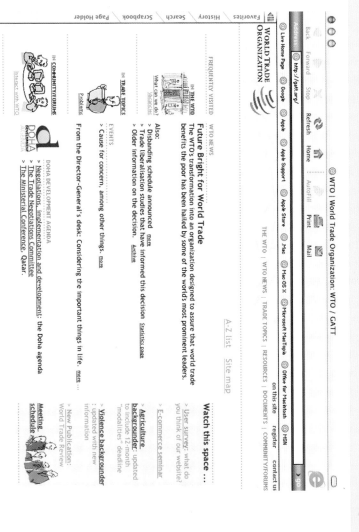

WORLD TRADE ORGANIZATION

Back | Forward | Stop | Refresh | Home | AutoFill | Print | Mail

Address: http://gatt.org/

WTO | World Trade Organization, WTO / GATT

Live Home Page | Google | Apple | Apple Support | Apple Store | Mac | Mac OS X | Microsoft MacTopia | Office for Macintosh | MSN

go

Favorites | History | Search | Scrapbook | Page Holder

THE WTO | WTO NEWS | TRADE TOPICS | RESOURCES | DOCUMENTS | COMMUNITY/FORUMS

on this site   register   contact us

A-Z list   Site map

FREQUENTLY VISITED

WTO NEWS

Future Bright for World Trade

The WTO's transformation into an organization designed to assure that world trade benefits the poor has been hailed by some of the world's most prominent leaders.

IN THE WTO
What can we do? Vacancies

Also:
> Disbanding schedule announced more
> Trade liberalisation studies that have informed this decision Statistics page
> Older information on the decision. Archive

IN TRADE TOPICS

EVENTS
> Cause for concern, among other things. more

From the Director-General's desk: Considering the important things in life. more ....

IN COMMUNITY/FORUMS

Interact with WTO

DOHA DEVELOPMENT AGENDA
> Negotiations, implementation and development: the Doha agenda
> The Trade Negotiations Committee
> The Ministerial Conference, Qatar.

Watch this space ...

> User survey: what do you think of our website?

> E-commerce seminar

> **Agriculture backgrounder:** updated to include 12-month "modalities" deadline

> **Violence backgrounder** : updated with new information

> New Publication: World Trade Review

Meeting schedule

Problems

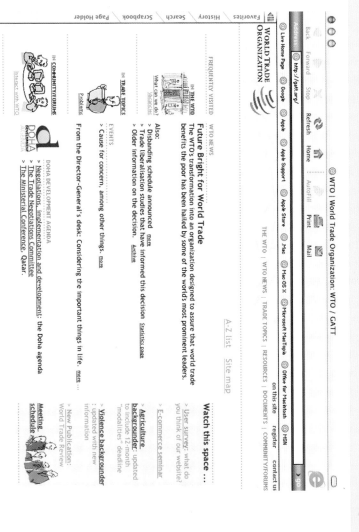

contact us World Trade Organization, rue de Lausanne 154, CH-1211 Geneva 21, Switzerland

But watch out: one of the sites below is full of misrepresentations, half-truths, and lies!

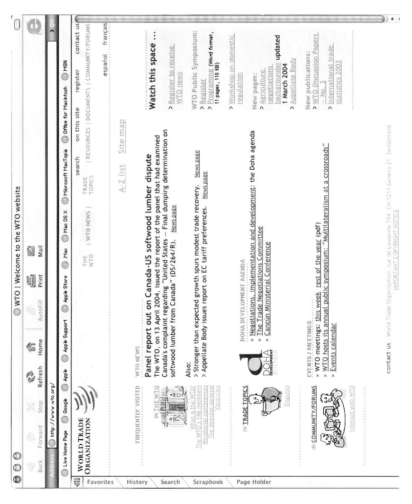

Photo / Image Credits

The Yes Men would like to thank all the artists who have kindly allowed us to reproduce their work. Our thanks to the creators of *The Yes Men* movie, stills from which appear throughout the book and are copyright 2004 Free Speech LLC. Every effort has been made to credit all copyright holders. We apologize for any errors or omissions.

p. 14 (photo of Patrick): B. Biamonte; pp. 56-57: Hemera Technologies, Inc.; p. 60: East Asia map copyright 1995-2002 Nova Development Corporation and its licensors. (all rights reserved); p. 62: Big Box of Art; pp. 68-69: Indymedia; p. 72: Indymedia; p. 75: Indymedia; p. 151(koala): Art Explosion 40,000; p. 152 (Sydney): Art Explosion 40,000; p. 154 (sheep): Art Explosion 40,000; p. 158 (New York City): Image Explosion; p. 164: Indymedia; p. 165 (corridor): Photodisc; p. 170 (dinner plate): Hemera Technologies Inc.

Also from The Disinformation Company

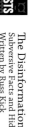

The Disinformation Book of Lists
Subversive Facts and Hidden Information in Rapid-Fire Format
Written by Russ Kick
Trade Paperback • 320 Pages • ISBN 0-9729529-4-2 • $16.95 (US)
In this book of surprising, subversive, and suppressed facts, Russ Kick crams maximum info into minimum space with lists including banned movies, botched executions, strange drugs, gay animals, illegal sex acts, secret nuclear tests and many more.

Uncovered: The Whole Truth about the Iraq War
Produced and Directed by Robert Greenwald
56 minutes + 34 minutes bonus footage • $9.95 (US)
The most controversial documentary since *Bowling for Columbine!* This DVD takes an arresting look at the speeches and spin given by the Bush Administration for the Iraq invasion. The time has come for truth to be heard.

Why Do People Hate America?
Written by Ziauddin Sardar and Merryl Wyn Davies
Trade Paperback • 240 Pages • ISBN 0-9713942-5-3 • $12.95 (US)
This international bestseller takes a close look at the consequences of interaction in a world in which gross disparities of power, wealth, freedom, and opportunity must be factored into each and every situation. An essential guide to understanding why Americans are targets and what causes hate.

50 Facts That Should Change The World
Written by Jessica Williams
Trade Paperback • 352 Pages • ISBN 0-9729529-6-9 • $14.95 (US)
A series of snapshots of life in the 21st century— these are the facts you need to know. Angry, polemic and often shocking; this is essential reading for anyone concerned about the state of the world today.

American Terminator
Myths, Movies, and Global Power
Written by Merryl Wyn Davies and Ziauddin Sardar
Trade Paperback • 240 Pages • ISBN 1-932857-01-X • $12.95 (US)
Takes on the dangerous fusion of the American Dream and American reality—one that many voters refuse to face. Fantasy politics at work in California become a blueprint for its failures overseas—a must read for those concerned with American democracy at home and abroad today.

disinformation®
The Disinformation Company Ltd.
http://www.disinfo.com